ΑΙΣΧΥΛΟΥ   AESCHYLUS'
Χοηφόροι   *Libation Bearers*

A Dual Language Edition

Greek Text Edited (1926) by
Herbert Weir Smyth

English Translation and Notes by
Ian Johnston

Edited by
Evan Hayes and Stephen Nimis

FAENUM PUBLISHING
OXFORD, OHIO

Aeschylus Libation Bearers: *A Dual Language Edition*
First Edition

© 2017 by Faenum Publishing

ISBN-10: 1940997852
ISBN-13: 9781940997858

Published by Faenum Publishing, Ltd.
Cover Design: Evan Hayes

for Geoffrey (1974-1997)

οἵη περ φύλλων γενεὴ τοίη δὲ καὶ ἀνδρῶν.
φύλλα τὰ μέν τ' ἄνεμος χαμάδις χέει, ἄλλα δέ θ' ὕλη
τηλεθόωσα φύει, ἔαρος δ' ἐπιγίγνεται ὥρη:
ὣς ἀνδρῶν γενεὴ ἣ μὲν φύει ἣ δ' ἀπολήγει.

Generations of men are like the leaves.
In winter, winds blow them down to earth,
but then, when spring season comes again,
the budding wood grows more. And so with men:
one generation grows, another dies away.   (*Iliad* 6)

TABLE OF CONTENTS

EDITORS' NOTE

This book presents the Greek text of Aeschylus' *Libation Bearers* with a facing English translation. The Greek text is that of Herbert Weir Smyth (1926), which is in the public domain and available as a pdf. This text has also been digitized by the Perseus Project (perseus.tufts.edu). The English translation and accompanying notes are those of Ian Johnston of Vancouver Island University, Nanaimo, BC. This translation is available freely online (records.viu.ca/~johnstoi/). We have reset both texts, making a number of very minor corrections, and placed them on opposing pages. This facing-page format will be useful to those wishing to read the English translation while looking at the Greek version, or vice versa.

Note that some discrepancies exists between the Greek text and English translation. Occasionally readings from other editions of or commentaries on Aeschylus' Greek text are used, accounting for some minor departures from Smyth.

Lecture on the *Oresteia*
by Ian Johnston

The following notes began as a lecture delivered, in part, at Malaspina College (now Vancouver Island University) in Liberal Studies 301 on September 25, 1995. That lecture was considerably revised in July 2000. This text is in the public domain, released July 2000. Note that references to Aeschylus's text are to the translation by Robert Fagles (Penguin, 1977).

Introduction

My lecture today falls into two parts. In the first I want to offer some background information for our study of Aeschylus's *Oresteia*, specifically on the Trojan War and the House of Atreus, and in the second I will be addressing the first play in that trilogy, the *Agamemnon*, making relatively brief mention of the other plays in the trilogy. Other speakers today will focus in more detail on the second and third plays.

The Trojan War

With the possible exception of the narratives in the Old Testament, no story has been such a fecund artistic resource in Western culture as the Greeks' favourite tale, the Trojan War. This is a vast, complex story, which includes a great many subsidiary narratives, and it has over the centuries proved an inexhaustible resource for Western writers, painters, musicians, choreographers, novelists, and dramatists. It would be comparatively easy and very interesting to develop a course of study of Western Culture based entirely upon artistic depictions of events from this long narrative. So it's an important part of cultural literacy for any students of our traditions to have some acquaintance with the details of this story, which even today shows no sign of losing its appeal.

There is not time here today to go into the narrative in any depth. So I'm going to be dealing only with a very brief treatment of those details most immediately pertinent to our study of Aeschylus. However, for those who want to go over a more comprehensive summary of the total narrative, see p. xxiii.

The complete narrative of the Trojan War includes at least six sections: the long-term causes (the Judgment of Paris), the immediate causes (the seduction of Helen of Troy by Paris), the preparations (especially the gathering of the forces at Aulis and the sacrifice of Iphigeneia), the events of the war (climaxing in the Wooden Horse and the destruction of the city), the returns (most notably the adventures of Odysseus and Aeneas and the murder of Agamemnon), and the long-term aftermath.

The total narrative is found by putting together many different versions, not all of which by any means agree on the details. Unlike the Old Testament narrative which was eventually codified into an official single version (at least for Christians and Jews), the story of the Trojan War exists in many versions of separate incidents in many different documents. There is no single authoritative account. Homer's *Iliad* and *Odyssey* enjoyed a unique authority in classical Greece, but those works deal only with a relatively small parts of the total narrative and are by no means the only texts which deal with the subject matter they cover.

Was the Trojan War a historical event or an endlessly embroidered fiction? The answer to this question is much disputed. The ancient Greeks believed in the historical truth of the tale and dated it at approximately 1200 BC, about the same time as the Exodus of the Israelites from Egypt. Until the last century, however, most later Europeans thought of the story as a poetic invention. This attitude changed quickly when a rich German merchant, Schliemann, in the nineteenth century, explored possible sites for the city (using Homeric geography as a clue) and unearthed some archeological remains of a city, one version of which had apparently been violently destroyed at about the traditional date. The site of this city, in Hissarlik in modern Turkey, is now widely believed to be the historical site of ancient Troy (although we cannot be certain).

What we need to know as background for Aeschylus's play is a comparatively small portion of this total narrative, which Aeschylus assumes his audience will be thoroughly familiar with. The expedition against Troy was initiated as a response to the seduction of Helen by Paris, a son of Priam, King of Troy, and their running off together back to Troy with a great quantity of Spartan treasure. Helen, the daughter of Zeus and Leda, was married to Menelaus, king of Sparta. His brother, Agamemnon, was king of Argos, married to Helen's twin sister Clytaemnestra (but whose father was not Zeus).

As a result of the abduction of Helen, the Greeks mounted an expedition against Troy, headed up by the two kings, Agamemnon and Menelaus, the sons of Atreus, or the Atreidai. They summoned their allies to meet them with troops at Aulis, where the ships were to take the troops on board and sail to Troy.

However, Agamemnon had angered the goddess Artemis by killing a sacred animal. So Artemis sent contrary winds, and the fleet could not sail. The entire expedition was threatened with failure. Finally, the prophet Calchas informed the Greek leadership that the fleet would not be able to sail unless

Agamemnon sacrificed his eldest daughter, Iphigeneia. He did so, and the fleet sailed to Troy, where, after ten years of siege, the city finally fell to the Greeks, who then proceeded to rape, pillage, and destroy the temples of the Trojans. The Greek leaders divided up the captive women. Agamemnon took Cassandra, a daughter of king Priam, home as a slave concubine. Cassandra had refused the sexual advances of the god Apollo; he had punished her by giving her the gift of divine prophecy but making sure that no one ever believed her.

The moral construction put on the Trojan War varies a good deal from one writer to the next. Homer's *Iliad*, for example, sees warfare as a condition of existence and therefore the Trojan War is a symbol for life itself, a life in which the highest virtues are manifested in a tragic heroism. In the *Odyssey*, there is a strong sense that the warrior life Odysseus has lived at Troy is something he must learn to abandon in favour of something more suited to home and hearth. Euripides used the stories of the war to enforce either a very strong anti-war vision or to promote highly unnaturalistic and ironic romance narratives.

In Aeschylus's play there is a strong sense that the Trojan War is, among other things, an appropriate act of revenge for the crime of Paris and Helen against Menelaus. And yet, at the same time, it is something which most of the people at home despise, for it kills all the young citizens and corrupts political life by taking the leaders away. In fact, the complex contradictions in the Chorus's attitude to that war help to bring out one of the major points of the first play: the problematic nature of justice based on a simple revenge ethic. According to the traditional conception of justice, Agamemnon is right to fight against Troy; but the effort is destroying his own city. So how can that be right?

The House of Atreus

The other background story which Aeschylus assumes his audience will be thoroughly familiar with is the story of the House of Atreus. This story, too, is recounted in more detail in the note on the Trojan War mentioned above.

The important point to know for the play is that the House of Atreus suffers from an ancient curse. As part of the working out of this curse, Agamemnon's father, Atreus, had quarreled violently with his brother Thyestes. As a result of this quarrel, Atreus had killed Thyestes's sons and fed them to him at a reconciliation banquet. In some versions of the story, Thyestes, overcome with horror, produced a child with his surviving daughter in order to have someone to avenge the crime. The offspring of that sexual union was Aegisthus (Aeschylus changes this point by having Aegisthus an infant at the time of the banquet). Aegisthus' actions in the *Oresteia*, the seduction of Clytaemnestra (before the play starts) and the killing of Agamemnon, he interprets and excuses as a revenge for what Atreus did to his father and brothers. (For a more detailed summary account of the story of the House of Atreus, see p. xxxv.)

The House of Atreus is probably the most famous secular family in our literary history, partly because it tells the story of an enormous family curse, full of sex, violence, horrible deaths going on for generations. It also throws into relief a theme which lies at the very centre of the *Oresteia* and which has intrigued our culture ever since, the nature of revenge.

The Revenge Ethic

Aechylus's trilogy, and especially the first play, calls our attention repeatedly to a central concept of justice: justice as revenge. This is a relatively simple notion, and it has a powerful emotional appeal, even today. The revenge ethic, simply put, makes justice the personal responsibility of the person insulted or hurt or, if that person is dead, of someone closely related to him, almost invariably a close blood relative. The killer must be killed, and that killing must be carried out personally by the most appropriate person, who accepts that charge as an obvious responsibility. It is a radically simple and powerfully emotional basis for justice, linking retribution to the family and their feelings for each other and for their collective honour.

We have already met this ethic in the Old Testament and in the *Odyssey*. In the latter book, the killing of Aegisthus by Orestes is repeatedly referred to with respect and approval: it was a just act because Aegisthus had violated Orestes's home and killed his father. And we are encouraged to see Odysseus's extraordinarily violent treatment of the suitors and their followers as a suitable revenge, as justice, for what they have done or tried to do to his household, especially his goods, his wife, and his son. Justice demands a personal, violent, and effective response from an appropriate family member.

And we are very familiar with this ethic from our own times, because justice as revenge seems to be an eternally popular theme of movies, televisions, books. It has become an integral part of the Western movie and of the police drama. Some actors create a career out of the genre (e.g., Charles Bronson and Arnold Swartzenegger and the Godfather).

We may not ourselves base our justice system directly and simply upon revenge, but we all understand very clearly those feelings which prompt a desire for revenge (especially when we think of any violence done to members of our own family), and we are often very sympathetic to those who do decide to act on their own behalf in meting out justice to someone who has killed someone near and dear to them.

So in reading the *Oresteia* we may be quite puzzled by the rather strange way the story is delivered to us, but there is no mistaking the importance or the familiarity of the issue. One way of approaching this play, in fact, is to see it primarily as an exploration of the adequacy of the revenge ethic as a proper basis for justice in the community and the movement towards a more civilized, effective, and rational way of judging crimes in the polis.

An Important Preliminary Interlude

Before going on to make some specific remarks about the *Agamemnon*, I'd like to call attention to an interpretative problem that frequently (too frequently) crops up with the *Oresteia*, especially among students, namely, the desire to treat this work as if it were, first and foremost, a philosophical investigation into concepts of justice rather than a great artistic fiction, a poetic exploration.

Why is this important? Well, briefly put, treating the play as if it were a rational argument on the order of, say, a Socratic enquiry, removes from our study of it the most important poetic qualities of the work. We concentrate all our discussions on the conceptual dimensions of the play, attending to the logic of Agamemnon's defense of his actions, or Clytaemnestra's of hers, or the final verdict of Athena in the trial of Orestes at the end, and we strive, above all, to evaluate the play on the basis of our response to the rational arguments put forward.

This approach is disastrous because the *Oresteia* is not a rational argument. It is, by contrast, an artistic exploration of conceptual issues. What matters here are the complex states of feeling which emerge from the characters, the imagery, the actions, and the ideas (as they are expressed by particular characters in the action). What we are dealing with here, in other words, is much more a case of how human beings feel about justice, about the possibilities for realizing justice in the fullest sense of the word within the human community, than a rational blueprint for implementing a new system.

I'll have more to say about this later, but let me give just one famous example. The conclusion of the trilogy will almost certainly create problems for the interpreter who seeks, above all else, a clearly worked out rational system for achieving justice in the community (understanding the rational justification for Athena's decision in the trial or the reconciliation with the Furies, for example, will be difficult to work out precisely). But Aeschylus, as a poet, is not trying to offer such a conclusion. What he gives us is a symbolic expression of our highest hopes, our most passionate desires for justice (which is so much more than a simple objective concept). The ending of the trilogy, with all those people (who earlier were bitter opponents) on stage singing and dancing in harmony, is a celebration of human possibility (and perhaps a delicate one at that), not the endorsement of a clearly codified system.

In the same way Athena's decision to acquit Orestes is not primarily the expression of a reasoned argument. It is far more an artistic symbol evocative of our highest hopes. This point needs to be stressed because (for understandable reasons) this part of the play often invites a strong feminist critique, as if what is happening here is the express desire to suppress feminine power. Now, I would be the last to deny the importance of the gendered imagery in the trilogy, but here I would also insist that Athena is a goddess, and her actions are, in effect, endorsing a shift in power from the divine to the human. Justice will no longer be a helpless appeal to the justice of Zeus in an endless sequence of killings: it will be the highest responsibility of the human community. The play does not "prove" that that's a good idea. It celebrates that as a possibility (and it may well be significant that that important hope is realized on stage by a divine power who is *female* but who is not caught up in the powerful nexus of the traditional family, since she sprung fully grown from Zeus' head).

This does not mean, I hasten to add, that we should abandon our reason as we approach the play. It does mean, however, that we must remain alert to the plays in the trilogy as works of art, and especially as dramatic works, designed to communicate their insights to us in performance. Yes, the plays deal with ideas, and we need to come to terms with those. But these ideas are never separate from human desires, motives, and passions. To see what Aeschylus is doing here, then, we need to look very carefully at all the various ways in which this emotional dimension, the full range of ambiguity and irony, establishes itself in the imagery, metaphors, and actions. We need, for example, always to be aware of how the way characters express their thoughts (especially the images they use) qualifies, complicates, and often undercuts the most obvious meanings of their words.

You will get a firm sense of what I mean if you consider that no one would ever put the *Oresteia* on a reading list for a philosophy course (except perhaps as background). Yet the work obviously belongs on any list of the world's great poetic dramas. We need to bear that in mind in our discussions, basing what we say on close readings of the text rather than on easy generalizations imposed on complex ironies.

Revenge in the Agamemnon

In the *Agamemnon*, revenge is the central issue. Agamemnon interprets his treatment of Troy as revenge for the crime of Paris and Helen; Clytaemnestra interprets her killing of Agamemnon as revenge for the sacrifice of Iphigeneia; Aegisthus interprets his role in the killing of Agamemnon as revenge for the treatment of his half-brothers by Agamemnon's father, Atreus. We are constantly confronted in this play with the realities of what revenge requires and what it causes, and we are always being asked to evaluate the justification for killing by appeals to the traditional revenge ethic.

But there's more to it than that. For in this play, unlike the *Odyssey*, revenge emerges as something problematic, something that, rather than upholding and restoring the polis, is threatening to engulf it in an unending cycle of destruction, until the most powerful city in the Greek world is full of corpses and vultures. In fact, one of the principal purposes of the first play of the trilogy is to force us to recognize that justice based on revenge creates special difficulties which it cannot solve. To use one of the most important images in the play, the city is caught in a net from which there seems to be no escape. The traditional revenge ethic has woven a cycle of necessary destruction around the city, and those caught in the mesh feel trapped in a situation they do not want but cannot alter.

The Chorus in the Agamemnon

The major way in which Aeschylus presents revenge to us as a problem in the *Agamemnon* is through the actions and the feelings of the Chorus. For us the huge part given to the Chorus is unfamiliar, and we may be tempted from time to time to skip a few pages until the next person enters, and the action moves forward. That is a major mistake, because following what is happening to the Chorus in the *Agamemnon* is essential to understanding the significance of what is going on. They provide all sorts of necessary background information, but, more important than that, they set the emotional and moral tone of the city. What they are, what they say, and how they feel represent the quality of life (in the full meaning of that term) available in the city.

First of all, who are these people? They are adult male citizens of Argos, those who ten years ago were too old to join the expedition to Troy. Hence, they are extremely old and very conscious of their own physical feebleness. And they are worried. They know the history of this family; they know very well about the sacrifice of Iphigeneia; and they have a very strong sense of what Clytaemnestra is about to do. They are full of an ominous sense of what is in store, and yet they have no means of dealing with that or even talking about it openly. Thus, in everything they say until quite near the end of the play, there is a very strong feeling of moral evasiveness: Agamemnon is coming home, and justice awaits. They know what that means. It is impossible to read very much of those long choruses without deriving a firm sense of their unease at what is going to happen and of their refusal and inability to confront directly the sources of that unease.

Why should this create problems for them? Well, they are caught in something of a dilemma. On the one hand, the only concept of justice they understand is the traditional revenge ethic: the killer must be killed. At the same time, they are weary of the slaughter. They are fearful for the future of their city, since the revenge ethic is destroying its political fabric. And they don't approve of what Clytaemnestra and Aegisthus are up to. They may sense that there's a certain "justice" in the revenge for Iphigeneia, but they are not satisfied that that is how things should be done, because Agamemnon, or someone like him, is necessary for the survival of the city.

In that sense their long account of the sacrifice of Iphigeneia is much more than simply narrative background. They are probing the past, searching through the sequence of events, as if somehow the justice of what has happened will emerge if they focus on the history which has led up to this point. But the effort gets them nowhere, and they are left with the desperately weak formulaic cry, "Let all go well," a repetitive prayer expressing a slim hope for a better future. They don't like what's happened in the past, but they cannot come to a mature acceptance of it, because it scares them. The actions of Agamemnon seem to fit the concept of justice, as they understand the term, but the actions themselves are horrific. They want it to make sense, but they cannot themselves derive any emotional satisfaction from the story or from what they suspect will happen next.

Thus, everything they utter up to the murder of Agamemnon is filled with a sense of moral unease and emotional confusion. They want the apparently endless cycle of retributive killings to stop, but they have no way of conceptualizing or imagining how that might happen. Their historical circumstances are too emotionally complex for the system of belief they have at hand to interpret the significance of those events. Since the only system of justice they have ever known tells them that the killings must continue and since they don't want them to continue, they are paralyzed. The physical weakness throughout much of the play is an obvious symbol for their moral and emotional paralysis. In fact, the most obvious thing about Argos throughout this first play is the moral duplicity and evasiveness of everyone in it.

This moral ambiguity of Argos manifests itself repeatedly in the way the Chorus and others refuse to reveal publicly what they are thinking and feeling. Right from the very opening of the play, in the Watchman's speech, what is for a brief moment an outburst of spontaneous joy at the news that Agamemnon will be returning is snuffed out with a prudent hesitancy and an admission that in Argos one does not dare utter one's thoughts. "I could tell you things if I wanted to," admits the Watchman, "but in this city an ox stands on my tongue."

The way in which the watchman's joy is instantly tempered by his guarded suspicion indicates, right at the very opening of the play, that we are in a murky realm here, where people are not free to state what they feel, where one feeling cancels out another, and where there's no sense of what anyone might do to resolve an unhappy situation.

It's important to note here that the political inertia of the old men of the chorus is not a function of their cowardice or their stupidity. They are neither of these. It comes from a genuine sense of moral and emotional confusion. As mentioned above, in order to understand their situation they are constantly reviewing the past, bringing to our attention the nature of the warfare in Troy (which they hate), the terrible destruction caused by Helen (whom they despise), the awful sacrifice of Iphigeneia (for whom they express great sympathy), and so on. The moral code they have inherited tells them that, in some way or another, all these things are just. But that violates their feelings. Revenge, they realize, is not achieving what justice in the community is supposed, above all else, to foster, a secure and fair life in the polis, an emotional satisfaction with our communal life together. On the contrary, it is destroying Argos and will continue to do so, filling its citizens with fear and anxiety.

This attitude reaches its highest intensity in the interview they have with Cassandra. She unequivocally confronts them with their deepest fears: that they will see Agamemnon dead. Their willed refusal to admit that they understand what she is talking about is not a sign of their stupidity--they know very well what she means. But they cannot admit that to themselves, because then they would have to do something about it, and they have no idea what they should or could do. If they do nothing, then perhaps the problem will go away. Maybe Agamemnon can take care of it. Or, put another way, before acting decisively, they need a reason to act. But the traditional reasons behind justice are telling them that they have no right to intervene.

The situation does not go away of course. Agamemnon is killed, and Clytaemnestra emerges to deliver a series of triumphant speeches over his corpse. It is particularly significant to observe what happens to the Chorus of old men at this point. They have no principled response to Clytaemnestra, but they finally are forced to realize that what has just happened is, in some fundamental way, a violation of what justice in the polis should be all about, and that they therefore should not accept it. And this emotional response rouses them to action: for the first time they openly defy the rulers of the city, at some risk to themselves. They have no carefully worked out political agenda, nor can they conceptualize what they are doing. Their response is radically emotional: the killing of the king must be wrong. Civil war is averted, because Clytaemnestra and Aegisthus do not take up the challenge, retiring to the palace. But the end of the *Agamemnon* leaves us with the most graphic image of a city divided against itself. What has gone on in the name of justice is leading to the worst of all possible communal disasters, civil war, the most alarming manifestation of the total breakdown of justice.

This ending is, in part, not unlike the ending of the *Odyssey*, where Odysseus's revenge against the suitors initiates a civil war between him and his followers and those whose duty it is to avenge the slain. But Homer does not pursue the potential problem of justice which this poses. Instead he wraps the story up quickly with a divine intervention, which forcibly imposes peace on the antagonists. We are thus not invited to question the justice of Odysseus's actions, which in any case have divine endorsement throughout.

In Aeschylus's first play, by contrast, the problems of a city divided against itself by the inadequacy of the revenge ethic become the major focus of the second and third plays, which seek to find a way through the impasse.

Agamemnon and Clytaemnestra

In contrast to the moral difficulties of the Chorus, the two main characters in the *Agamemnon*, Agamemnon and Clytaemnestra, have no doubts about what justice involves: it is based upon revenge. And the two of them act decisively in accordance with the old ethic to destroy those whom the code decrees must be destroyed, those whom they have a personal responsibility to hurt in the name of vengeance for someone close to them.

Now, in accordance with that old revenge code, both of them have a certain justification for their actions (which they are not slow to offer). But Aeschylus's treatment of the two brings out a very important limitation of the revenge ethic, namely the way in which it is compromised by the motivation of those carrying out justice.

For in spite of their enmity for each other, Agamemnon and Clytaemnestra have some obvious similarities. They live life to satisfy their own immediate desires for glory and power, and to gratify their immoderate passions, particularly their blood lust. Whatever concerns they have for the polis take second place to the demands of their own passionate natures. They do not suffer the same moral anguish as the Chorus because they feel powerful enough to act on how they feel and because their very strong emotions about themselves are not in the slightest tempered by a sense of what is best for the city or for anyone else. Their enormously powerful egos insist that they don't have to attend to anyone else's opinion (the frequency of the personal pronouns "I," "me," "mine," and "my" in their speech is really significant). They answer only to themselves.

More than this, the way in which each of the two main characters justifies the bloody revenge carried out in the name of justice reveals very clearly that they revel in blood killing. Shedding blood with a maximum of personal savagery, without any limit, gratifies each of them intensely, so much so that their joy in destruction calls into question their veracity in talking of themselves as agents of justice.

This is so pronounced a feature of these heroic figures that the play puts a certain amount of pressure on us to explore their motivation. They both claim they act in order to carry out justice. But do they? What other motives have come into play? When Agamemnon talks of how he obliterated Troy or walks on the red carpet or Clytaemnestra talks with delight about what a sexual charge she is going to get by making love to Aegisthus on top of the dead body of Agamemnon, we are surely invited to see that, however much they justify their actions with appeals to divine justice, their motivation has become very muddied with other, less noble motives.

Such observations may well occasion some dispute among interpreters. But in order to address them we need to pay the closest possible attention to the language and the motivation of these characters (as that is revealed in the language), being very careful not to accept too quickly the justifications they offer for their own actions. We need to ask ourselves repeatedly: On the basis of the language, how am I to understand the reasons why Agamemnon killed Iphigeneia and wiped out Troy? Why does Clytaemnestra so enjoy killing Agamemnon? If a disinterested sense of justice is all that is in play here, they why does she so enjoy killing Cassandra? Why, for that matter, does Agamemnon talk about the total destruction of Troy with such grim pleasure? Why does he get so much joy in talking about how he is going to bring justice back to Argos with a sword?

And this, I take it, is for Aeschylus a very important limitation on the revenge ethic. It brings into play concerns which have, on the face of it, no immediate connections with justice and everything to do with much baser human instincts. People like Agamemnon and Clytaemnestra, who claim (after the fact) to kill in the name of justice, actually are carrying out the destruction to satisfy much deeper, more urgent, and far less worthy human urges (a fact which may account for the fact that in their killing they go to excess, well beyond the strict demands of justice).

For that reason, Aeschylus gives us a very close look at the characters of Clytaemnestra and Agamemnon. As I say, we need to pay the closest attention to their language, trying to get a handle, not just on the surface details of what they are saying, but on the emotional complexities of the character uttering the lines. We need to ask ourselves the key question: In acting the way they do and for the reasons they state or reveal to us in their language, are they being just? Or is their sense of justice merely a patina covering something else? Or are both possibilities involved?

For instance, Clytaemnestra states that she killed Agamemnon in order to avenge Iphigeneia. Is that true? If it is a reason, how important is it? What else is involved here? In the second play, she confronts Orestes with this justification. But what is our response right at the moment after she has just done the deed? One needs here not merely to look at what she says but at how she says it. What particular emotions is she revealing in her style of speech and what do these reveal about her motives?

Such questions become all the more important when we compare how they set about their acts of "justice" with the opening of the second play, when we see Orestes return to carry out the next chapter in the narrative of the House of Atreus. For there's a really marked difference between his conduct and that of his parents. A great deal of the second play is taken up with Orestes' preparations to carry out his vision of justice. It's not unimportant that much of that time he's questioning himself, seeking advice from others, involving others publicly in what he feels he has to do. In a sense, he is trying to purge himself of those emotions which drive Agamemnon and Clytaemnestra to their acts of "justice," to make himself an agent of divine justice rather than serving his own blood-lust.

This, I take it, is a key element in Aeschylus's treatment of the theme of justice. So long as the revenge ethic rests in the hands of people like Agamemnon and Clytaemnestra, tragically passionate egotists who answer only to their own immediate desires, the cycle of killing will go on for ever, and cities will destroy themselves in the blood feud. The only way out (and it is a hope) is that someone like Orestes will act out of a love of justice as a divine principle, setting aside as best he can (or even acting against) his deepest, most irrational blood feelings, thus moving beyond the revenge ethic.

We will get little sense of why Orestes deserves to be declared innocent unless we attend very carefully to the difference between his motives and those of his parents, for it is surely an important element in Athena's final judgment that the traditional revenge ethic, as embodied in the Furies and manifested in the conduct of Agamemnon, Clytaemnestra, and Aegisthus, is no longer compatible with justice in the community and that Orestes' actions in killing his mother are, as much as he can make them, undertaken in the service of others (Apollo and the community), rather than stemming from a passionate blood-lust (the fact that Orestes is willing to stand trial and abide by the verdict is one important sign of the difference between him and his parents).

A Final Postscript

Human beings think about justice as a rational concept, institutionalized in their communities, but they also have strong emotions about justice, both within the family and the community. The revenge ethic harnessed to those powerful feelings in Aechylus's play stands exposed as something that finally violates our deepest sense of any possibility for enduring justice in our community, for it commits us a never-ending cycle of retributive killing and over-killing.

The *Oresteia* ends with a profound and very emotionally charged hope that the community can move beyond such a personally powerful emotional basis for justice and, with the sanction of the divine forces of the world, establish a system based on group discussion, consensus, juries (through what Athena calls persuasion)--in a word, can unite a conceptual, reasonable understanding of justice with our most powerful feelings about it. This work is, as Swinburne observed, one of the most optimistic visions of human life ever written, for it celebrates a dream we have that human beings in their communities can rule themselves justly, without recourse to blood vengeance, satisfying mind and heart in the process.

At the same time, however, Aeschylus is no shallow liberal thinker telling us to move beyond our brutal and unworkable traditions. For he understands that we cannot by some sleight of hand remove the Furies from our lives. They are ancient goddesses, eternally present. Hence, in the conclusion of the play the Furies, traditional goddesses of vengeance, are incorporated into the justice system, not excluded. And the powers they are given are significant: no city can thrive without them. Symbolically, the inclusion of the Furies in the final celebration, their new name (meaning "The Kindly Ones"), and their agreement fuse in a great theatrical display elements which were in open conflict only a few moments before.

It's as if the final image of this play stresses for us that in our justice we must strive to move beyond merely personal emotion (the basis of personal revenge) towards some group deliberations, but in the new process we must not violate our personal feelings or forget they have their role to play. If justice is to be a matter of persuasion, it cannot violate the deepest feelings we have (and have always had) about justice. If such violation takes place, the city will not thrive.

Every time I read the conclusion of this great trilogy, I think of how we nowadays may well have lost touch with that great insight: that justice is not just a matter of reasonable process and debate but also a matter of feeling. For a city to thrive justice must not only be reasonably done but must be felt to be done. Once our system starts to violate our feelings for justice, our city does not thrive. The Furies will see to that.

THE LEGEND OF THE TROJAN WAR
by Ian Johnston

This summary, which has been prepared by Ian Johnston of Malaspina University-College, Nanaimo, BC (now Vancouver Island University), for students in Classics 101 and Liberal Studies, is a brief account of a number of different old stories about the Trojan war, arranged in more or less chronological sequence. There are several different, even contradictory, versions of events. There is no one authoritative narrative of the whole war. Many of these stories were obviously current before Homer, and the story continued to be embellished by the Romans and Medieval writers]

1. The gods Apollo and Poseidon, during a time when they were being punished by having to work among men, built the city of Troy for Priam's father, Laomedon. They invited the mortal man Aeacus (the son of Zeus and Aegina and grandfather of Achilles) to help them, since destiny had decreed that Troy would one day be captured in a place built by human hands (so a human being had to help them).

2. When newly constructed, Troy was attacked and captured by Herakles (Hercules), Telamon (brother of Peleus and therefore the uncle of Achilles and father of Telamonian Ajax and Teucros), and Peleus (son of Aeacus and father of Achilles), as a punishment for the fact that Laomedon had not given Hercules a promised reward of immortal horses for rescuing Laomedon's daughter Hesione. Telamon killed Laomedon and took Hesione as a concubine (she was the mother of Teucros).

3. Priam, King of Troy and son of Laomedon, had a son from his wife Hekabe (or Hecuba), who dreamed that she had given birth to a flaming torch. Cassandra, the prophetic daughter of Priam, foretold that the new-born son, Paris (also called Alexandros or Alexander), should be killed at birth or else he would destroy the city. Paris was taken out to be killed, but he was rescued by shepherds and grew up away from the city in the farms by Mount Ida. As a young man he returned to Troy to compete in the athletic games, was recognized, and returned to the royal family.

4. Peleus (father of Achilles) fell in love with the sea nymph Thetis, whom Zeus, the most powerful of the gods, also had designs upon.

But Zeus learned of an ancient prophecy that Thetis would give birth to a son greater than his father, so he gave his divine blessing to the marriage of Peleus, a mortal king, and Thetis. All the gods were invited to the celebration, except, by a deliberate oversight, Eris, the goddess of strife. She came anyway and brought a golden apple, upon which was written "For the fairest." Hera (Zeus's wife), Aphrodite (Zeus's daughter), and Athena (Zeus's daughter) all made a claim for the apple, and they appealed to Zeus for judgment. He refused to adjudicate a beauty contest between his wife and two of his daughters, and the task of choosing a winner fell to Paris (while he was still a herdsman on Mount Ida, outside Troy). The goddesses each promised Paris a wonderful prize if he would pick her: Hera offered power, Athena offered military glory and wisdom, and Aphrodite offered him the most beautiful woman in the world as his wife. In the famous Judgement of Paris, Paris gave the apple to Aphrodite.

5. Helen, daughter of Tyndareus and Leda, was also the daughter of Zeus, who had made love to Leda in the shape of a swan (she is the only female child of Zeus and a mortal). Her beauty was famous throughout the world. Her father Tyndareus would not agree to any man's marrying her, until all the Greeks warrior leaders made a promise that they would collectively avenge any insult to her. When the leaders made such an oath, Helen then married Menelaus, King of Sparta. Her twin (non-divine) sister Klytaimnestra (Clytaemnestra), born at the same time as Helen but not a daughter of Zeus, married Agamemnon, King of Argos, and brother of Menelaus. Agamemnon was the most powerful leader in Hellas (Greece).

6. Paris, back in the royal family at Troy, made a journey to Sparta as a Trojan ambassador, at a time when Menelaus was away. Paris and Helen fell in love and left Sparta together, taking with them a vast amount of the city's treasure and returning to Troy via Cranae, an island off Attica, Sidon, and Egypt, among other places. The Spartans set off in pursuit but could not catch the lovers. When the Spartans learned that Helen and Paris were back in Troy, they sent a delegation (Odysseus, King of Ithaca, and Menelaus, the injured husband) to Troy demanding the return of Helen and the treasure. When the Trojans refused, the Spartans appealed to the oath which Tyndareus had forced them all to take (see 5 above), and the Greeks assembled an army to invade Troy, asking all the allies to meet in preparation for embarkation at Aulis. Some stories claimed that the real Helen never went to Troy, for she was carried off to Egypt by the god Hermes, and Paris took her double to Troy.

7. Achilles, the son of Peleus and Thetis, was educated as a young man by Chiron, the centaur (half man and half horse). One of the conditions of Achilles's parents' marriage (the union of a mortal with a divine sea nymph) was that the son born to them would die in war and bring great sadness to his mother. To protect him from death in battle his mother bathed the infant in the waters of the river Styx, which conferred invulnerability to any weapon. And when the Greeks began to assemble an army, Achilles's parents hid him at Scyros disguised as a girl. While there he met Deidameia, and they had a son Neoptolemos (also called Pyrrhus). Calchas, the prophet with the Greek army, told Agamemnon and the other leaders that they could not conquer Troy without Achilles. Odysseus found Achilles by tricking him; Odysseus placed a weapon out in front of the girls of Scyros, and Achilles reached for it, thus revealing his identity. Menoitios, a royal counsellor, sent his son Patroclus to accompany Achilles on the expedition as his friend and advisor.

8. The Greek fleet of one thousand ships assembled at Aulis. Agamemnon, who led the largest contingent, was the commander-in-chief. The army was delayed for a long time by contrary winds, and the future of the expedition was threatened as the forces lay idle. Agamemnon had offended the goddess Artemis by an impious boast, and Artemis had sent the winds. Finally, in desperation to appease the goddess, Agamemnon sacrificed his daughter Iphigeneia. Her father lured her to Aulis on the pretext that she was to be married to Achilles (whose earlier marriage was not known), but then he sacrificed her on the high altar. One version of her story claims that Artemis saved her at the last minute and carried her off to Tauris where she became a priestess of Artemis in charge of human sacrifices. While there, she later saved Orestes and Pylades. In any case, after the sacrifice Artemis changed the winds, and the fleet sailed for Troy.

9. On the way to Troy, Philoctetes, the son of Poeas and leader of the seven ships from Methone, suffered a snake bite when the Greeks landed at Tenedos to make a sacrifice. His pain was so great and his wound so unpleasant (especially the smell) that the Greek army abandoned him against his will on the island.

10. The Greek army landed on the beaches before Troy. The first man ashore, Protesilaus, was killed by Hector, son of Priam and leader of the Trojan army. The Greeks sent another embassy to Troy, seeking to recover Helen and the treasure. When the Trojans denied them, the Greek army settled down into a siege which lasted many years.

11. In the tenth year of the war (where the narrative of the *Iliad* begins), Agamemnon insulted Apollo by taking as a slave-hostage the girl Chryseis, the daughter of Chryses, a prophet of Apollo, and refusing to return her when her father offered compensation. In revenge, Apollo sent nine days of plague down upon the Greek army. Achilles called an assembly to determine what the Greeks should do. In that assembly, he and Agamemnon quarrelled bitterly, Agamemnon confiscated from Achilles his slave girl Briseis, and Achilles, in a rage, withdrew himself and his forces (the Myrmidons) from any further participation in the war. He asked his mother, Thetis, the divine sea nymph, to intercede on his behalf with Zeus to give the Trojans help in battle, so that the Greek forces would recognize how foolish Agamemnon had been to offend the best soldier under his command. Thetis made the request of Zeus, reminding him of a favour she had once done for him, warning him about a revolt against his authority, and he agreed.

12. During the course of the war, numerous incidents took place, and many died on both sides. Paris and Menelaus fought a duel, and Aphrodite saved Paris just as Menelaus was about to kill him. Achilles, the greatest of the Greek warriors, slew Cycnus, Troilus, and many others. He also, according to various stories, was a lover of Patroclus, Troilus, Polyxena, daughter of Priam, Helen, and Medea. Odysseus and Diomedes slaughtered thirteen Thracians (Trojan allies) and stole the horses of King Rhesus in a night raid. Telamonian Ajax (the Greater Ajax) and Hector fought a duel with no decisive result. A common soldier, Thersites, challenged the authority of Agamemnon and demanded that the soldiers abandon the expedition. Odysseus beat Thersites into obedience. In the absence of Achilles and following Zeus's promise to Thetis (see 11), Hector enjoyed great success against the Greeks, breaking through their defensive ramparts on the beach and setting the ships on fire

13. While Hector was enjoying his successes against the Greeks, the latter sent an embassy to Achilles, requesting him to return to battle. Agamemnon offered many rewards in compensation for his initial insult (see 11). Achilles refused the offer but did say that he would reconsider if Hector ever reached the Greek ships. When Hector did so, Achilles's friend Patroclus (see 7) begged to be allowed to return to the fight. Achilles gave him permission, advising Patroclus not to attack the city of Troy itself. He also gave Patroclus his own suit of armour, so that the Trojans might think that Achilles had returned to the war. Patroclus resumed the fight, enjoyed some dazzling success

(killing one of the leaders of the Trojan allies, Sarpedon from Lykia), but he was finally killed by Hector, with the help of Apollo.

14. In his grief over the death of his friend Patroclus, Achilles decided to return to the battle. Since he had no armour (Hector had stripped the body of Patroclus and had put on the armour of Achilles), Thetis asked the divine artisan Hephaestus, the crippled god of the forge, to prepare some divine armour for her son. Hephaestus did so, Thetis gave the armour to Achilles, and he returned to the war. After slaughtering many Trojans, Achilles finally cornered Hector alone outside the walls of Troy. Hector chose to stand and fight rather than to retreat into the city, and he was killed by Achilles, who then mutilated the corpse, tied it to his chariot, and dragged it away. Achilles built a huge funeral pyre for Patroclus, killed Trojan soldiers as sacrifices, and organized the funeral games in honour of his dead comrade. Priam travelled to the Greek camp to plead for the return of Hector's body, and Achilles relented and returned it to Priam in exchange for a ransom.

15. In the tenth year of the war the Amazons, led by Queen Penthesilea, joined the Trojan forces. She was killed in battle by Achilles, as was King Memnon of Ethiopa, who had also recently reinforced the Trojans. Achilles's career as the greatest warrior came to an end when Paris, with the help of Apollo, killed him with an arrow which pierced him in the heel, the one vulnerable spot, which the waters of the River Styx had not touched because his mother had held him by the foot (see 7) when she had dipped the infant Achilles in the river. Telamonian Ajax, the second greatest Greek warrior after Achilles, fought valiantly in defense of Achilles's corpse. At the funeral of Achilles, the Greeks sacrificed Polyxena, the daughter of Hecuba, wife of Priam. After the death of Achilles, Odysseus and Telamonian Ajax fought over who should get the divine armour of the dead hero. When Ajax lost the contest, he went mad and committed suicide. In some versions, the Greek leaders themselves vote and decide to award the armour to Odysseus.

16. The Greeks captured Helenus, a son of Priam, and one of the chief prophets in Troy. Helenus revealed to the Greeks that they could not capture Troy without the help of Philoctetes, who owned the bow and arrows of Hercules and whom the Greeks had abandoned on Tenedos (see 9 above). Odysseus and Neoptolemus (the son of Achilles) set out to persuade Philoctetes, who was angry at the Greeks for leaving him alone on the island, to return to the war, and by trickery they

succeeded. Philoctetes killed Paris with an arrow shot from the bow of Hercules.

17. Odysseus and Diomedes ventured into Troy at night, in disguise, and stole the Palladium, the sacred statue of Athena, which was supposed to give the Trojans the strength to continue the war. The city, however, did not fall. Finally the Greeks devised the strategy of the wooden horse filled with armed soldiers. It was built by Epeius and left in front of Troy. The Greek army then withdrew to Tenedos (an island off the coast), as if abandoning the war. Odysseus went into Troy disguised, and Helen recognized him. But he was sent away by Hecuba, the wife of Priam, after Helen told her. The Greek soldier Sinon stayed behind when the army withdrew and pretended to the Trojans that he had deserted from the Greek army because he had information about a murder Odysseus had committed. He told the Trojans that the horse was an offering to Athena and that the Greeks had built it to be so large that the Trojans could not bring it into their city. The Trojan Laocoon warned the Trojans not to believe Sinon ("I fear the Greeks even when they bear gifts"); in the midst of his warnings a huge sea monster came from the surf and killed Laocoon and his sons.

18. The Trojans determined to get the Trojan Horse into their city. They tore down a part of the wall, dragged the horse inside, and celebrated their apparent victory. At night, when the Trojans had fallen asleep, the Greek soldiers hidden in the horse came out, opened the gates, and gave the signal to the main army which had been hiding behind Tenedos. The city was totally destroyed. King Priam was slaughtered at the altar by Achilles's son Neoptolemos. Hector's infant son, Astyanax, was thrown off the battlements. The women were taken prisoner: Hecuba (wife of Priam), Cassandra (daughter of Priam), and Andromache (wife of Hector). Helen was returned to Menelaus.

19. The gods regarded the sacking of Troy and especially the treatment of the temples as a sacrilege, and they punished many of the Greek leaders. The fleet was almost destroyed by a storm on the journey back. Menelaus's ships sailed all over the sea for seven years—to Egypt (where, in some versions, he recovered his real wife in the court of King Proteus—see 6 above). Agamemnon returned to Argos, where he was murdered by his wife Clytaemnestra and her lover, Aegisthus. Cassandra, whom Agamemnon had claimed as a concubine after the destruction of Troy, was also killed by Clytaemnestra. Aegisthus was seeking revenge for what the father of Agamemnon (Atreus) had

done to his brother (Aegisthus' father) Thyestes. Atreus had given a feast for Thyestes in which he fed to him the cooked flesh of his own children (see the family tree of the House of Atreus given below). Clytaemnestra claimed that she was seeking revenge for the sacrifice of her daughter Iphigeneia (see 8 above).

20. Odysseus (called by the Romans Ulysses) wandered over the sea for many years before reaching home. He started with a number of ships, but in a series of misfortunes, lasting ten years because of the enmity of Poseidon, the god of the sea, he lost all his men before returning to Ithaca alone. His adventures took him from Troy to Ismareos (land of the Cicones); to the land of the Lotos Eaters, the island of the cyclops (Poseidon, the god of the sea, became Odysseus's enemy when Odysseus put out the eye of Polyphemus, the cannibal cyclops, who was a son of Poseidon); to the cave of Aeolos (god of the winds), to the land of the Laestrygonians, to the islands of Circe and Calypso, to the underworld (where he talked to the ghost of Achilles); to the land of the Sirens, past the monster Scylla and the whirlpool Charybdis, to the pastures of the cattle of Helios, the sun god, to Phaiacia. Back in Ithaca in disguise, with the help of his son Telemachus and some loyal servants, he killed the young princes who had been trying to persuade his wife, Penelope, to marry one of them and who had been wasting the treasure of the palace and trying to kill Telemachus. Odysseus proved who he was by being able to string the famous bow of Odysseus, a feat which no other man could manage, and by describing for Penelope the secret of their marriage bed, that Odysseus had built it around an old olive tree.

21. After the murder of Agamemnon by his wife Clytaemnestra (see 19 above), his son Orestes returned with a friend Pylades to avenge his father. With the help of his sister Electra (who had been very badly treated by her mother, left either unmarried or married to a poor farmer so that she would have no royal children), Orestes killed his mother and Aegisthus. Then he was pursued by the Furies, the goddesses of blood revenge. Suffering fits of madness, Orestes fled to Delphi, then to Tauri, where, in some versions, he met his long-lost sister, Iphigeneia. She had been rescued from Agamemnon's sacrifice by the gods and made a priestess of Diana in Tauri. Orestes escaped with Iphigeneia to Athens. There he was put on trial for the matricide. Apollo testified in his defense. The jury vote was even; Athena cast the deciding vote in Orestes's favour. The outraged Furies were placated by being given a permanent place in Athens and a certain authority in the judicial process. They were then renamed the Eumenides (The

Kindly Ones). Orestes was later tried for the same matricide in Argos, at the insistence of Tyndareus, Clytaemnestra's father. Orestes and Electra were both sentenced to death by stoning. Orestes escaped by capturing Helen and using her as a hostage.

22. Neoptolemus, the only son of Achilles, married Hermione, the only daughter of Helen and Menelaus. Neoptolemus also took as a wife the widow of Hector, Andromache. There was considerable jealously between the two women. Orestes had wished to marry Hermione; by a strategy he arranged it so that the people of Delphi killed Neoptolemus. Then he carried off Hermione and married her. Menelaus tried to kill the son of Neoptolemus, Molossus, and Andromache, but Peleus, Achilles's father, rescued them. Andromache later married Helenus. Orestes's friend Pylades married Electra, Orestes sister.

23. Aeneas, the son of Anchises and the goddess Aphrodite and one of the important Trojan leaders in the Trojan War, fled from the city while the Greeks were destroying it, carrying his father, Anchises, his son Ascanius, and his ancestral family gods with him. Aeneas wandered all over the Mediterranean. On his journey to Carthage, he had an affair with Dido, Queen of Carthage. He abandoned her without warning, in accordance with his mission to found another city. Dido committed suicide in grief. Aeneas reached Italy and there fought a war against Turnus, the leader of the local Rutulian people. He did not found Rome but Lavinium, the main centre of the Latin league, from which the people of Rome sprang. Aeneas thus links the royal house of Troy with the Roman republic.

The Cultural Influence of the Legend of the Trojan War

No story in our culture, with the possible exception of the Old Testament and the story of Jesus Christ, has inspired writers and painters over the centuries more than the Trojan War. It was the fundamental narrative in Greek education (especially in the version passed down by Homer, which covers only a small part of the total narrative), and all the tragedians whose works survive wrote plays upon various aspects of it, and these treatments, in turn, helped to add variations to the traditional story. No one authoritative work defines all the details of the story outlined above.

Unlike the Old Testament narratives, which over time became codified in a single authoritative version, the story of the Trojan War exists as a large collection of different versions of the same events (or parts of them). The war has been interpreted as a heroic tragedy, as a fanciful romance, as a satire against warfare, as a love story, as a passionately anti-war tale, and so on. Just as there is no single version which defines the "correct" sequence of events, so there is no single interpretative slant on how one should understand the war. Homer's poems enjoyed a unique authority, but they tell only a small part of the total story.

The following notes indicate only a few of the plays, novels, and poems which have drawn on and helped to shape this ancient story.

1.   The most famous Greek literary stories of the war are Homer's *Iliad* and *Odyssey*, our first two epic poems, composed for oral recitation probably in the eighth century before Christ. The theme of the *Iliad* is the wrath of Achilles at the action of Agamemnon, and the epic follows the story of Achilles' withdrawal from the war and his subsequent return (see paragraphs 11, 12, 13, and 14 above). The *Odyssey* tells the story of the return of Odysseus from the war (see 20 above). A major reason for the extraordinary popularity and fecundity of the story of the Trojan War is the unquestioned quality and authority of these two great poems, even though they tell only a small part of the total narrative and were for a long time unavailable in Western Europe (after they were lost to the West, they did not appear until the fifteenth century). The *Iliad* was the inspiration for the archaeological work of Schliemann in the nineteenth century, a search which resulted in the discovery of the site of Troy at Hissarlik, in modern Turkey.

2.   The Greek tragedians, we know from the extant plays and many fragments, found in the story of the Trojan War their favorite material, focusing especially on the events after the fall of the city. Aeschylus's famous trilogy, *The Oresteia* (*Agamemnon*, *Choephoroi* [*Libation Bearers*], and *Eumenides* [*The Kindly Ones*]), tells of the murder of Agamemnon and Cassandra by Clytaemnestra and Aegisthus, the revenge of Orestes, and the trial for the matricide. Both Sophocles and Euripides wrote plays about Electra, and Euripides also wrote a number of plays based on parts the larger story: *The Trojan Women*, *The Phoenissae*, *Orestes*, *Helen*, and *Iphigeneia in Tauris* (see 21 and 22 above). Sophocles also wrote *Philoctetes* (see 16) and *Ajax* (see 15) on events in the Trojan War.

3.   Greek philosophers and historians used the Trojan War as a common example to demonstrate their own understanding of human conduct. So Herodotus and Thucydides, in defining their approach to the historical past, both offer an analysis of the origins of the war. Plato's *Republic* uses many parts of Homer›s epics to establish important points about political wisdom (often citing Homer as a negative

example). Alexander the Great carried a copy of the *Iliad* around with him in a special royal casket which he had captured from Darius, King of the Persians.

4. The Romans also adopted the story. Their most famous epic, Virgil's *Aeneid*, tells the story of Aeneas (see 23). And in the middle ages, the Renaissance, and right up to the present day, writers have retold parts of the ancient story. These adaptations often make significant changes in the presentation of particular characters, notably Achilles, who in many versions becomes a knightly lover, and Odysseus/Ulysses, who is often a major villain. Ulysses and Diomedes appear in Dante's *Inferno*. Of particular note are Chaucer's and Shakespeare's treatments of the story of Troilus and Cressida.

    Modern writers who have drawn on the literary tradition of this ancient cycle of stories include Sartre (*The Flies*), O'Neill (*Mourning Becomes Electra*), Giradoux (*Tiger at the Gates*), Joyce (*Ulysses*), Eliot, Auden, and many others. In addition, the story has formed the basis for operas and ballets, and the story of *Odysseus* has been made into a mini-series for television. This tradition is a complicated one, however, because many writers, especially in Medieval times, had no direct knowledge of the Greek sources and re-interpreted the details in very non-Greek ways (e.g., Dante, Chaucer, and Shakespeare). Homer's text, for example, was generally unknown in Western Europe until the late fifteenth century.

5. For the past two hundred years there has been a steady increase in the popularity of Homer's poems (and other works dealing with parts of the legend) translated into English. Thus, in addition to the various modern adaptations of parts of the total legend of the Trojan war (e.g., Brad Pitt's *Troy*), the ancient versions are still very current.

The Royal House of Atreus

The most famous (or notorious) human family in Western literature is the House of Atreus, the royal family of Mycenae. To follow the brief outline below, consult the simplified family tree on p. xxv. Note that different versions of the story offer modifications of the family tree.

The family of Atreus suffered from an ancestral crime, variously described. Most commonly Tantalus, son of Zeus and Pluto, stole the food of the gods. In another version he kills his son Pelops and feeds the flesh to the gods (who later, when they discover what they have eaten, bring Pelops back to life). Having eaten the food of the gods, Tantalus is immortal and so cannot be killed. In Homer's *Odyssey*, Tantalus is punished everlastingly in the underworld.

The family curse originates with Pelops, who won his wife Hippodamia in a chariot race by cheating and betraying and killing his co-conspirator (who, as he was drowning, cursed the family of Pelops). The curse blighted the next generation: the brothers Atreus and Thyestes quarrelled. Atreus killed Thyestes's sons and served them to their father at a reconciliation banquet.

To obtain revenge, Thyestes fathered a son on his surviving child, his daughter Pelopia. This child was Aegisthus, whose task it was to avenge the murder of his brothers. When Agamemnon set off for Troy (sacrificing his daughter Iphigeneia so that the fleet could sail from Aulis), Aegisthus seduced Clytaemnestra and established himself as a power in Argos.

When Agamemnon returned, Clytaemnestra and Aegisthus killed him (and his captive Cassandra)--Aegisthus in revenge for his brothers, Clytaemnestra in revenge for the sacrifice of Iphigeneia. Orestes at the time was away, and Electra had been disgraced.

Orestes returned to Argos to avenge his father. With the help of a friend, Pylades, and his sister Electra, he succeeded by killing his mother, Clytaemnestra, and her lover, Aegisthus. After many adventures (depending upon the narrative) he finally received absolution for the matricide, and the curse was over.

Many Greek poets focused on this story. Homer repeatedly mentions the murder of Agamemnon in the *Odyssey* and the revenge of Orestes on Aegisthus (paying no attention to the murder of Clytaemnestra); Aeschylus's great trilogy *The Oresteia* is the most famous classical treatment of the tale; Sophocles and Euripides both wrote plays on Orestes and Electra.

One curious note is the almost exact parallel between the story of Orestes in this family tale and the story of *Hamlet*. These two stories arose, it seems, absolutely independently of each other, and yet in many crucial respects are extraordinarily similar. This match has puzzled many a comparative literature scholar and invited all sorts of psychological theories about the trans-cultural importance of matricide as a theme.

For a more detailed account of the House of Atreus, see the following section.

THE HOUSE OF ATREUS:
A Note on the Mythological Background to the *Oresteia*
by Ian Johnston

Introduction

The following paragraphs provide a brief summary of the major events in the long history of the House of Atreus, one of the most fecund and long-lasting of all the Greek legends. Like so many other stories, the legend of the House of Atreus varies a good deal from one author to the next and there is no single authoritative version. The account given below tries to include as many of the major details as possible. At the end there is a short section reviewing Aeschylus' treatment of the story in the *Oresteia*.

Family Tree (Simplified)

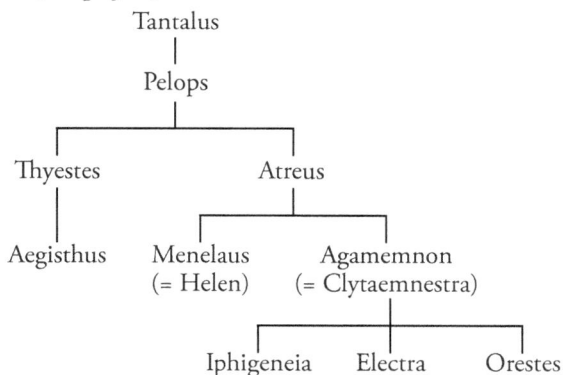

```
                        Tantalus
                           |
                        Pelops
            ┌──────────────┴──────────────┐
        Thyestes                        Atreus
            |                   ┌──────────┴──────────┐
        Aegisthus           Menelaus              Agamemnon
                           (= Helen)          (= Clytaemnestra)
                                       ┌───────────┼───────────┐
                                   Iphigeneia   Electra     Orestes
```

1. The family of Atreus (father of Agamemnon and Menelaus) traces its origins back to Tantalus, king of Sipylos, a son of Zeus (famous for his eternal punishment in Hades, as described in the *Odyssey*, where he is always thirsty but can never drink, hence the origin of the word *tantalizing*). Tantalus had a son called Pelops, whom Poseidon loved.

2. Pelops wished to marry Hippodameia, daughter of king Oenomaus. Oenomaus set up a contest (a chariot race against the king) for all those who wished to woo his daughter. If the suitor lost, he was killed. A number of men had died in such a race before Pelops made his attempt. Pelops bribed the king's charioteer (Myrtilus) to disable the

king's chariot. In the race, Oenomaus' chariot broke down (the wheels came off), and the king was killed. Pelops then carried off Hippodameia as his bride. Pelops also killed his co-conspirator Myrtilus by throwing him into the sea. Before he drowned Myrtilus (in some versions Oenomaus) cursed Pelops and his family. This act is the origin of the famous curse on the House of Atreus.

3. Pelops does not seems to have been affected by the curse. He had a number of children, the most important of whom were his two sons, the brothers Atreus and Thyestes. Atreus married Aerope, and they had two sons, Agamemnon and Menelaus. And Thyestes had two sons and a daughter Pelopia.

4. Atreus and Thyestes quarrelled (in some versions at the instigation of the god Hermes, father of Myrtilus, the charioteer killed by Pelops). Thyestes had an affair with Atreus' wife, Aerope, and was banished from Argos by Atreus. However, Thyestes petitioned to be allowed to return, and Atreus, apparently wishing a reconciliation, agreed to allow Thyestes to come back and prepared a huge banquet to celebrate the end of their differences.

5. At the banquet, however, Atreus served Thyestes the cooked flesh of Thyestes' two slaughtered sons. Thyestes ate the food, and then was informed of what he had done. This horrific event is the origin of the term *Thyestean Banquet*. Overcome with horror, Thyestes cursed the family of Atreus and left Argos with his one remaining child, his daughter Pelopia.

6. Some versions of the story include the name Pleisthenes, a son of Atreus who was raised by Thyestes. To become king, Thyestes sent Pleisthenes to kill Atreus, but Atreus killed him, not realizing he was killing his son. This, then, becomes another cause of the quarrel. In yet other accounts, someone called Pleisthenes is the first husband of Aerope and the father of Agamemnon and Menelaus. When he died, so this version goes, Atreus married Aerope and adopted her two sons. In Aeschylus' play there is one reference to Pleisthenes; otherwise, this ambiguous figure is absent from the story.

7. In some versions, including Aeschylus' account, Thyestes had one small infant son who survived the banquet, Aegisthus. In other accounts, however, Aegisthus was the product of Thyestes' incestuous relationship with his daughter Pelopia after the murder of the two older sons, conceived especially to be the avenger of the notorious banquet.

8. Agamemnon and Menelaus, the two sons of Atreus, married Clytaemnestra and Helen respectively, two twin sisters, but not identical twins (Clytaemnestra had a human father; whereas, Helen was a daughter of Zeus). Helen was so famous for her beauty that a number of men wished to marry her. The suitors all agreed that they would act to support the man she eventually married in the event of any need for mutual assistance. Agamemnon and Clytaemnestra had three children, Iphigeneia, Orestes, and Electra.

9. When Helen (Menelaus' wife) ran off to Troy with Paris, Agamemnon and Menelaus organized and led the Greek forces against the Trojans. The army assembled at Aulis, but the fleet could not sail because of contrary winds sent by Artemis. Agamemnon sacrificed his daughter Iphigeneia in order to placate Artemis.

10. With Agamemnon and Menelaus off in Troy, Aegisthus (son of Thyestes) returned to Argos, where he became the lover of Clytaemnestra, Agamemnon's wife. They sent Orestes into exile, to live with an ally, Strophius in Phocis, and humiliated Electra, Agamemnon's surviving daughter (either treating her as a servant or marrying her off to a common farmer). When Agamemnon returned, the two conspirators successfully killed him and assumed royal control of Argos.

11. Orestes returned from exile and, in collaboration with his sister Electra, avenged his father by killing Clytaemnestra and Aegisthus. In many versions this act makes him lose his self-control and he becomes temporarily deranged. He then underwent ritual purification by Apollo and sought refuge in the temple of Athena in Athens. There he was tried and acquitted. This action put the curses placed on the House of Atreus to rest.

Some Comments

The story of the House of Atreus, and particularly Orestes' and Electra's revenge for their father's murder, is one of the most popular and enduring of all Greek legends, a favourite among the classical tragedians and still very popular with modern playwrights (e.g., T. S. Eliot, Eugene O'Neill, Jean Paul Sartre). However, different writers tell the story in very different ways.

Homer, for example (in the *Odyssey*) sets up Orestes' killing of Aegisthus as an entirely justified way to proceed (Homer ascribes the main motivation and planning to Aegisthus, who has to persuade Clytaemnestra to agree and who, it seems, does the actual killing). In fact, the action is repeatedly mentioned as a clear indication of divinely supported justice (there is no direct mention of the killing of Clytaemnestra, although there is a passing reference to Orestes' celebrations over his "hateful" mother after the killing of Aegisthus). Sophocles and Euripides tell basically the same story but with enormously different depictions of the main characters (in Euripides' version Orestes and Electra are hateful; whereas, in Sophocles' *Electra* they are much more conventionally righteous).

Aeschylus confines his attention to Atreus' crime against his brother (the Thyestean banquet) and what followed from it. There is no direct reference to Thyestes' adultery with Atreus' wife (although Cassandra makes a reference to a man sleeping with his brother's wife) or to any events from earlier parts of the story (unless the images of chariot racing are meant to carry an echo of Pelops' actions). This has the effect of making Atreus' crime against his brother the origin of the family curse (rather than the actions of Pelops or Tantalus) and tends to give the reader more sympathy for Aegisthus than some other versions do.

Curiously enough, Orestes' story has many close parallels with the Norse legend on which the story of Hamlet is based (son in exile is called upon to avenge a father killed by the man who has seduced his mother, perhaps with the mother's consent; the son carries out the act of killing his mother and her lover with great difficulty, undergoing fits of madness, and so on). Given that there is no suggestion of any possible literary-historical link between the origin of these two stories, the similarity of these plots offers a number of significant problems for psychologists and mythologists to explore. This puzzle is especially intriguing because the Hamlet-Orestes narrative is by far the most popular story in the history of English dramatic tragedy.

ΧΟΗΦΟΡΟΙ

LIBATION BEARERS

ΤΑ ΤΟΥ ΔΡΑΜΑΤΟΣ ΠΡΟΣΩΠΑ

Ορεστης

Χορος

Ηλεκτρα

Οικετης

Κλυταιμνηστρα

Πυλαδης

Τροφος

Αιγισθος

DRAMATIS PERSONAE

ORESTES: son of Agamemnon and Clytaemnestra, brother of Electra.

CHORUS: slave women captured at Troy and serving the royal palace at Argos.

ELECTRA: daughter of Agamemnon and Clytaemnestra, sister of Orestes.

SERVANT: house slave serving in the royal palace.

CLYTAEMNESTRA: widow of Agamemnon, lover of Aegisthus, mother of Orestes and Electra.

PYLADES: friend of Orestes.

CILISSA: Orestes' old nurse, a servant in the palace.

AEGISTHUS: son of Thyestes, lover of Clytaemnestra.[1]

ATTENDANTS on Orestes and Pylades and Aegisthus.

Χοηφόροι

ΟΡΕΣΤΗΣ

Ἑρμῆ χθόνιε, πατρῷ᾽ ἐποπτεύων κράτη,
σωτὴρ γενοῦ μοι ξύμμαχός τ᾽ αἰτουμένῳ·
ἥκω γὰρ ἐς γῆν τήνδε καὶ κατέρχομαι.
τύμβου δ᾽ ἐπ᾽ ὄχθῳ τῷδε κηρύσσω πατρὶ
κλύειν, ἀκοῦσαι .   .   .   5
. . . . .
.   .   . πλόκαμον Ἰνάχῳ θρεπτήριον.
τὸν δεύτερον δὲ τόνδε πενθητήριον
. . . . .
οὐ γὰρ παρὼν ᾤμωξα σόν, πάτερ, μόρον
οὐδ᾽ ἐξέτεινα χεῖρ᾽ ἐπ᾽ ἐκφορᾷ νεκροῦ.
. . . . .
τί χρῆμα λεύσσω; τίς ποθ᾽ ἥδ᾽ ὁμήγυρις   10
στείχει γυναικῶν φάρεσιν μελαγχίμοις
πρέπουσα; ποίᾳ ξυμφορᾷ προσεικάσω;
πότερα δόμοισι πῆμα προσκυρεῖ νέον;
ἢ πατρὶ τὠμῷ τάσδ᾽ ἐπεικάσας τύχω
χοὰς φερούσας νερτέροις μειλίγματα;   15
οὐδέν ποτ᾽ ἄλλο· καὶ γὰρ Ἠλέκτραν δοκῶ
στείχειν ἀδελφὴν τὴν ἐμὴν πένθει λυγρῷ
πρέπουσαν. ὦ Ζεῦ, δός με τείσασθαι μόρον
πατρός, γενοῦ δὲ σύμμαχος θέλων ἐμοί.
Πυλάδη, σταθῶμεν ἐκποδών, ὡς ἂν σαφῶς   20
μάθω γυναικῶν ἥτις ἥδε προστροπή.

4

The Libation Bearers

Scene: Argos, the tomb of Agamemnon some years after his murder by Clytaemnestra and Aegisthus. Behind the tomb stands the royal palace of the sons of Atreus.

[Enter Orestes and Pylades. They have just arrived in Argos]

ORESTES

    Hermes, messenger to the dead, guardian
    of your father's powers, help rescue me—
    work with me, I beg you, now I've come back,
    returned to this land from exile.[2] On this grave,
    on this heaped-up earth, I call my father,
    imploring him to listen, to hear me . . .

[Orestes cuts two locks of his hair and sets them one by one on the tomb]

    Here's a lock of hair, offering to Inachus,
    the stream where I was raised. Here's another,
    a token of my grief. I was not there,
    my father, to mourn your death. I couldn't stretch
    my hand out to you, when they carried off
    your corpse for burial.

[Enter Electra and the Chorus, dressed in black. They do not see Orestes and Pylades]

                       What's this I see?   [10]
    What's this crowd of women coming here,
    all wearing black in public? What does it mean?
    What new turn of fate? Has some fresh sorrow
    struck the house? Or am I right to think
    they bring libations here to honour you,
    my father, to appease the dead below?
    That must be it. I see my sister there,
    Electra. That's her approaching with them.
    She's grieving—in great pain—that's obvious.
    O Zeus, let me avenge my father's death.
    Support me as my ally in this fight.
    Pylades, let's stand over there and hide,   [20]
    so I can find out what's taking place,
    what brings these suppliant women here.

5

Aeschylus

ΧΟΡΟΣ
 ἰαλτὸς ἐκ δόμων ἔβαν
 χοὰς προπομπὸς ὀξύχειρι σὺν κτύπῳ.
 πρέπει παρηὶς φοινίοις ἀμυγμοῖς
 ὄνυχος ἄλοκι νεοτόμῳ·   25
 δι' αἰῶνος δ' ἰυγμοῖσι βόσκεται κέαρ.
 λινοφθόροι δ' ὑφασμάτων
 λακίδες ἔφλαδον ὑπ' ἄλγεσιν,
 προστέρνῳ στολμῷ
 πέπλων ἀγελάστοις   30
 ξυμφοραῖς πεπληγμένων.

 τορὸς δὲ Φοῖβος ὀρθόθριξ
 δόμων ὀνειρόμαντις, ἐξ ὕπνου κότον
 πνέων, ἀωρόνυκτον ἀμβόαμα
 μυχόθεν ἔλακε περὶ φόβῳ,   35
 γυναικείοισιν ἐν δώμασιν βαρὺς πίτνων.
 κριταί <τε> τῶνδ' ὀνειράτων
 θεόθεν ἔλακον ὑπέγγυοι
 μέμφεσθαι τοὺς γᾶς
 νέρθεν περιθύμως   40
 τοῖς κτανοῦσί τ' ἐγκοτεῖν.

 τοιάνδε χάριν ἀχάριτον ἀπότροπον κακῶν,
 ἰὼ γαῖα μαῖα,
 μωμένα μ' ἰάλλει   45
 δύσθεος γυνά. φοβοῦ-
 μαι δ' ἔπος τόδ' ἐκβαλεῖν.
 τί γὰρ λύτρον πεσόντος αἵματος πέδοι;
 ἰὼ πάνοιζυς ἑστία,
 ἰὼ κατασκαφαὶ δόμων.   50
 ἀνήλιοι βροτοστυγεῖς
 δνόφοι καλύπτουσι δόμους
 δεσποτῶν θανάτοισι.

6

[Orestes and Pylades conceal themselves from the sight of Electra and the Chorus]

CHORUS
    I've been sent here from the palace,
    to bring libations for the dead,
    to clap out the hands' sharp beat.
    Blood flows down my cheeks
    from cuts my nails have scratched.
    As life drags on and on, my heart
    feeds itself on my laments,
    to the sound of garments torn apart,
    the sound of sorrow in our clothes,
    as we rip the woven linen
    covering our breasts.
    No laughter any more.   [30]
    Our fortune beats us down.

    With hair-raising shrieks, Fear,
    dream-prophet in this house,
    breathed a furious cry of terror,
    at night, while people were asleep.
    Deep within the inner house
    the heavy scream re-echoed, all the way
    to rooms where women slept.
    Those who read our dreams,
    who speak by heaven's will,
    declared, "The dead beneath the ground   [40]
    are discontent—their anger grows
    against the ones who killed them."

    O Earth, my mother Earth,
    to protect herself from harm
    that godless woman sends me here
    with gifts, with loveless gifts.
    But I'm too scared to speak her words,
    the prayer she wishes me to say.
    What can atone for blood
    once fallen on the ground?
    Alas for the grief-filled hearth,
    Alas for the buried home!   [50]
    Sunless darkness grips the house
    which all men hate, for now
    their master's murdered.

σέβας δ᾽ ἄμαχον ἀδάματον ἀπόλεμον τὸ πρὶν   55

δι᾽ ὤτων φρενός τε

δαμίας περαῖνον

νῦν ἀφίσταται. φοβεῖ-

ται δέ τις. τὸ δ᾽ εὐτυχεῖν,

τόδ᾽ ἐν βροτοῖς θεός τε καὶ θεοῦ πλέον.   60

ῥοπὴ δ᾽ ἐπισκοπεῖ δίκας

ταχεῖα τοὺς μὲν ἐν φάει,

τὰ δ᾽ ἐν μεταιχμίῳ σκότου

μένει χρονίζοντας ἄχη [βρύει],

τοὺς δ᾽ ἄκραντος ἔχει νύξ.   65

δι᾽ αἵματ᾽ ἐκποθένθ᾽ ὑπὸ χθονὸς τροφοῦ

τίτας φόνος πέπηγεν οὐ διαρρύδαν.

διαλγὴς ⟨δ᾽⟩ ἄτα διαφέρει

τὸν αἴτιον παναρκέτας νόσου βρύειν.   70

θιγόντι δ᾽ οὔτι νυμφικῶν ἑδωλίων

ἄκος, πόροι τε πάντες ἐκ μιᾶς ὁδοῦ

⟨προ⟩βαίνοντες τὸν χερομυσῆ

φόνον καθαίροντες ἴθυσαν μάταν.

ἐμοὶ δ᾽ —ἀνάγκαν γὰρ ἀμφίπολιν   75

θεοὶ προσήνεγκαν· (ἐκ γὰρ οἴκων

πατρῴων δούλιόν ⟨μ᾽⟩ ἐσᾶγον αἶσαν)—

δίκαια καὶ μὴ δίκαια ἀρχὰς πρέπον

βίᾳ φρενῶν αἰνέσαι   80

πικρὸν στύγος κρατούσῃ.

δακρύω δ᾽ ὑφ᾽ εἱμάτων

8

It's gone—that ancient splendour
no man could resist or fight,
no man could overcome.
Its glory rang in every ear,
echoed in every heart.
Now it's been thrown away.
But each man feels the fear.
For now, in all men's eyes,
success is worshipped,   [60]
more so than god himself.
But Justice is vigilant—
she tips the scales.
With some she's quick,
striking by light of day,
for others sorrows wait,
delaying until their lives
are half way sunk in twilight,
while others are embraced
by night that never ends.

The nurturing earth drinks blood,
she drinks her fill. That gore,
which cries out for revenge,
will not dissolve or seep away.
The guilty live in utter desperation—
madness preys upon their minds
infecting them completely.   [70]

The man who violates a virgin's bed
cannot be redeemed. All rivers flow
into one stream to cleanse his hand
of black blood which defiles him.
Such waters flow in vain.

As for me—gods set a fatal noose
around my city, so I was led
out of my father's house a slave.
Now I do what I have to do—
beat down my bitter rage.
Against my inclinations,   [80]
I follow what my masters say,
whether right or wrong.
Still, behind our veils
we weep for her, this girl,

9

Aeschylus

ματαίοισι δεσποτᾶν
τύχαις, κρυφαίοις πένθεσιν παχνουμένη.

ἨΛΕΚΤΡΑ

δμωαὶ γυναῖκες, δωμάτων εὐθήμονες,
ἐπεὶ πάρεστε τῆσδε προστροπῆς ἐμοὶ   85
πομποί, γένεσθε τῶνδε σύμβουλοι πέρι·
τί φῶ χέουσα τάσδε κηδείους χοάς;
πῶς εὔφρον’ εἴπω, πῶς κατεύξομαι πατρί;
πότερα λέγουσα παρὰ φίλης φίλῳ φέρειν
γυναικὸς ἀνδρί, τῆς ἐμῆς μητρὸς πάρα;   90
τῶνδ’ οὐ πάρεστι θάρσος, οὐδ’ ἔχω τί φῶ,
χέουσα τόνδε πέλανον ἐν τύμβῳ πατρός.
ἢ τοῦτο φάσκω τοὔπος, ὡς νόμος βροτοῖς,
ἔσθλ’ ἀντιδοῦναι τοῖσι πέμπουσιν τάδε
στέφη, δόσιν γε τῶν κακῶν ἐπαξίαν;   95

ἢ σῖγ’ ἀτίμως, ὥσπερ οὖν ἀπώλετο
πατήρ, τάδ’ ἐκχέασα, γάποτον χύσιν,
στείχω καθάρμαθ’ ὥς τις ἐκπέμψας πάλιν
δικοῦσα τεῦχος ἀστρόφοισιν ὄμμασιν;

τῆσδ’ ἐστὲ βουλῆς, ὦ φίλαι, μεταίτιαι·   100
κοινὸν γὰρ ἔχθος ἐν δόμοις νομίζομεν.
μὴ κεύθετ’ ἔνδον καρδίας φόβῳ τινός.
τὸ μόρσιμον γὰρ τόν τ’ ἐλεύθερον μένει
καὶ τὸν πρὸς ἄλλης δεσποτούμενον χερός.
λέγοις ἄν, εἴ τι τῶνδ’ ἔχοις ὑπέρτερον.   105

ΧΟΡΟΣ

αἰδουμένη σοι βωμὸν ὡς τύμβον πατρὸς
λέξω, κελεύεις γάρ, τὸν ἐκ φρενὸς λόγον.

ἨΛΕΚΤΡΑ

λέγοις ἄν, ὥσπερ ἠδέσω τάφον πατρός.

ΧΟΡΟΣ

φθέγγου χέουσα κεδνὰ τοῖσιν εὔφροσιν.

her senseless suffering,
as grief, concealed and cold,
congeals our hearts to ice.

ELECTRA
You women who keep our house in order,
now you're here attending me in prayers,
in supplication, give me your advice.
What should I say as I pour out these cups,
my offering to grief? How frame my words
to make my prayer a tribute to my father?
Shall I say I bring these gifts with love,
from doting wife to her beloved husband,   [90]
from my mother? I have no strength for that.
I don't know what to say, as I pour out
this oil and honey on my father's tomb.
Shall I recite the words men often use,
"May those who send this noble tribute
get back the same." No, let him give them
a gift their treachery deserves! Or should I
stand here in silence and dishonour, the way
my father died, empty out these cups,
with eyes averted as I toss the gift,
let the earth drink, and then retrace my steps,
like someone sent to carry out the trash
left over from some purifying rite?
Help me, my friends, with your advice.   [100]
We share a common hatred in the house.
Don't hide what's in your hearts. Don't be afraid
of anyone. Fate waits for each of us—
the free and those in bondage to another.
Speak up, if you can think of something better.

CHORUS LEADER
I respect your father's tomb, as if it were
an altar. So I'll speak straight from my heart,
as you have asked.

ELECTRA
                              Then talk to me,
out of your reverence for my father's grave.

CHORUS LEADER
As you pour, bless those who are your friends.

ΗΛΕΚΤΡΑ

τίνας δὲ τούτους τῶν φίλων προσεννέπω;   110

ΧΟΡΟΣ

πρῶτον μὲν αὐτὴν χὤστις Αἴγισθον στυγεῖ.

ΗΛΕΚΤΡΑ

ἐμοί τε καὶ σοί τἄρ' ἐπεύξομαι τάδε;

ΧΟΡΟΣ

αὐτὴ σὺ ταῦτα μανθάνουσ' ἤδη φράσαι.

ΗΛΕΚΤΡΑ

τίν' οὖν ἔτ' ἄλλον τῇδε προστιθῶ στάσει;

ΧΟΡΟΣ

μέμνησ' Ὀρέστου, κεἰ θυραῖός ἐσθ' ὅμως.   115

ΗΛΕΚΤΡΑ

εὖ τοῦτο, κἀφρένωσας οὐχ ἥκιστά με.

ΧΟΡΟΣ

τοῖς αἰτίοις νῦν τοῦ φόνου μεμνημένη—

ΗΛΕΚΤΡΑ

τί φῶ; δίδασκ' ἄπειρον ἐξηγουμένη.

ΧΟΡΟΣ

ἐλθεῖν τιν' αὐτοῖς δαίμον' ἢ βροτῶν τινα—

ΗΛΕΚΤΡΑ

πότερα δικαστὴν ἢ δικηφόρον λέγεις;   120

ΧΟΡΟΣ

ἁπλῶς τι φράζουσ', ὅστις ἀνταποκτενεῖ.

ΗΛΕΚΤΡΑ

καὶ ταῦτά μούστὶν εὐσεβῆ θεῶν πάρα;

ΧΟΡΟΣ

πῶς δ' οὐ τὸν ἐχθρὸν ἀνταμείβεσθαι κακοῖς;

ELECTRA
Of those close to me, whom shall I call friends?   [110]

CHORUS LEADER
First, name yourself—then anyone
who hates Aegisthus.

ELECTRA
                              Then I'll make this prayer
on my own behalf. Shall I include you too?

CHORUS LEADER
That's your decision. In this ritual
you must let your judgment guide you.

ELECTRA
Who else should I then add to join with us?

CHORUS LEADER
He may be far from home, but don't forget Orestes.

ELECTRA
That's good. You give me excellent advice.

CHORUS LEADER
Remember, too, the guilty murderers.

ELECTRA
What do I say? I've never practised this.
Teach me what I should say.

CHORUS LEADER
                              Let some god
or mortal man come down on them.

ELECTRA
You mean as judge or as avenger? Which?   [120]

CHORUS LEADER
Pronounce these words—and clearly—
"Someone who'll pay back life by taking life."

ELECTRA
Is it a righteous thing for me to do,
to petition gods like that?

CHORUS
                              Why not?
How can it not be a righteous thing to pray
to pay back one's enemies for evil?

13

ἨΛΕΚΤΡΑ

κῆρυξ μέγιστε τῶν ἄνω τε καὶ κάτω,   124
<ἄρηξον,> Ἑρμῆ χθόνιε, κηρύξας ἐμοὶ   124a
τοὺς γῆς ἔνερθε δαίμονας κλύειν ἐμὰς   125
εὐχάς, πατρῴων δωμάτων ἐπισκόπους,
καὶ Γαῖαν αὐτήν, ἣ τὰ πάντα τίκτεται,
θρέψασά τ' αὖθις τῶνδε κῦμα λαμβάνει·
κἀγὼ χέουσα τάσδε χέρνιβας βροτοῖς
λέγω καλοῦσα πατέρ', 'ἐποίκτιρόν τ' ἐμὲ   130
φίλον τ' Ὀρέστην· πῶς ἀνάξομεν δόμοις;
πεπραμένοι γὰρ νῦν γέ πως ἀλώμεθα
πρὸς τῆς τεκούσης, ἄνδρα δ' ἀντηλλάξατο
Αἴγισθον, ὅσπερ σοῦ φόνου μεταίτιος.
κἀγὼ μὲν ἀντίδουλος· ἐκ δὲ χρημάτων   135
φεύγων Ὀρέστης ἐστίν, οἱ δ' ὑπερκόπως
ἐν τοῖσι σοῖς πόνοισι χλίουσιν μέγα.
ἐλθεῖν δ' Ὀρέστην δεῦρο σὺν τύχῃ τινὶ
κατεύχομαί σοι, καὶ σὺ κλῦθί μου, πάτερ·
αὐτῇ τέ μοι δὸς σωφρονεστέραν πολὺ   140
μητρὸς γενέσθαι χεῖρά τ' εὐσεβεστέραν.

ἡμῖν μὲν εὐχὰς τάσδε, τοῖς δ' ἐναντίοις
λέγω φανῆναί σου, πάτερ, τιμάορον,
καὶ τοὺς κτανόντας ἀντικατθανεῖν δίκῃ.
ταῦτ' ἐν μέσῳ τίθημι τῆς καλῆς ἀρᾶς,   145
κείνοις λέγουσα τήνδε τὴν κακὴν ἀράν·
ἡμῖν δὲ πομπὸς ἴσθι τῶν ἐσθλῶν ἄνω,
σὺν θεοῖσι καὶ γῇ καὶ δίκῃ νικηφόρῳ.'

τοιαῖσδ' ἐπ' εὐχαῖς τάσδ' ἐπισπένδω χοάς.
ὑμᾶς δὲ κωκυτοῖς ἐπανθίζειν νόμος,   150
παιᾶνα τοῦ θανόντος ἐξαυδωμένας.

ΧΟΡΟΣ

ἵετε δάκρυ καναχὲς ὀλόμενον
ὀλομένῳ δεσπότᾳ
πρὸς ἔρυμα τόδε κακῶν, κεδνῶν τ'

ELECTRA

    Oh Hermes, mighty herald, moving
    between earth above and earth below,
    messenger to the dead, assist me now—
    summon the spirits there beneath the ground
    who guard my father's house, to hear my prayers.
    And call on Earth herself, who, giving birth
    and nurturing all things, in due course takes back
    the swollen tide of their increasing store.
    As I pour out these offering to the dead,
    I call upon my father, "Pity me—   [130]
    and dear Orestes, too! How can we rule
    in our own home? We're beggars now,
    as if our mother traded us away,
    exchanged us for her mate, Aegisthus,
    her partner in your murder. For now I live
    just like a slave. Orestes lives in exile,
    far from his estates. In their arrogance,
    those two squander all the wealth you worked for.
    And so I pray to you—dear father,
    let good fortune bring Orestes home!
    Father, hear me. Make me more self-controlled,   [140]
    than mother, my hand more righteous!
    Those are my prayers for us. Our enemies—
    for them, my father, I pray someone will come
    as your avenger, then kill your killers,
    in retribution, as is just. As I pray
    for our well being, I include this curse—
    may they be caught by their own evil.
    Bring us your blessing to the earth above,
    with help from gods, and Earth, and Justice,
    all combined to bring us victory."

[Electra pours out her libation on the tomb]

    Those are my prayers, and over them I pour
    libations. Your duty now is to lament,
    to crown my prayers with flowers, chanting   [150]
    your mournful chorus for the dead.

CHORUS

    Come, let our tears begin,
    fall, and die, as our master died.
    Let them guard us from evil,

ἀπότροπον ἄγος ἀπεύχετον   155

κεχυμένων χοᾶν. κλύε δέ μοι, κλύε, σέ-

βας ὦ δέσποτ᾽, ἐξ ἀμαυρᾶς φρενός.

ὀτοτοτοτοτοτοτοῖ,

ἴτω τις δορυ-

σθενὴς ἀνήρ, ἀναλυτὴρ δόμων,   160

Σκυθικά τ᾽ ἐν χεροῖν παλίντον᾽

ἐν ἔργῳ βέλη ᾽πιπάλλων Ἄρης

σχέδιά τ᾽ αὐτόκωπα νωμῶν ξίφη.

ΗΛΕΚΤΡΑ

ἔχει μὲν ἤδη γαπότους χοὰς πατήρ·

νέου δὲ μύθου τοῦδε κοινωνήσατε·   165

ΧΟΡΟΣ

λέγοις ἄν· ὀρχεῖται δὲ καρδία φόβῳ.

ΗΛΕΚΤΡΑ

ὁρῶ τομαῖον τόνδε βόστρυχον τάφῳ.

ΧΟΡΟΣ

τίνος ποτ᾽ ἀνδρός, ἢ βαθυζώνου κόρης;

ΗΛΕΚΤΡΑ

εὐξύμβολον τόδ᾽ ἐστὶ παντὶ δοξάσαι.   170

ΧΟΡΟΣ

πῶς οὖν; παλαιὰ παρὰ νεωτέρας μάθω.

ΗΛΕΚΤΡΑ

οὐκ ἔστιν ὅστις πλὴν ἐμοῦ κείραιτό νιν.

ΧΟΡΟΣ

ἐχθροὶ γὰρ οἷς προσῆκε πενθῆσαι τριχί.

16

preserve the good, and keep away
with our outpoured libations
the polluting curse.
Hear me, oh hear me,
my honoured master.
May your disembodied spirit
hear my prayer.

Alas, alas . . . ohhhhhhhh!
Let him come now,   [160]
some forceful man,
a power with the spear.
May he restore this house,
bent Scythian bow in hand,
a fist around his sword hilt.
Like Ares, god of war,
let him begin the slaughter!

ELECTRA

My father's now received his offerings.
The earth has drunk them up. But look—
here's something new. Come, look at it with me.

CHORUS

Speak up. My heart's afraid. It's dancing.

ELECTRA

I see a lock of hair, an offering . . . on the tomb.

CHORUS

Whose is it? A man's? A full-grown girl's?

ELECTRA

It shouldn't be too difficult to guess,   [170]
to sort out what this indicates.

CHORUS

How so? Let your youth instruct your elders.

ELECTRA

No one but me could have cut this off.

CHORUS

You're right. Those who should make offerings,
cutting their hair in grief, are enemies.

ἨΛΕΚΤΡΑ
καὶ μὴν ὅδ᾽ ἐστὶ κάρτ᾽ ἰδεῖν ὁμόπτερος—

ΧΟΡΟΣ
ποίαις ἐθείραις; τοῦτο γὰρ θέλω μαθεῖν.   175

ἨΛΕΚΤΡΑ
αὐτοῖσιν ἡμῖν κάρτα προσφερὴς ἰδεῖν.

ΧΟΡΟΣ
μῶν οὖν Ὀρέστου κρύβδα δῶρον ἦν τόδε;

ἨΛΕΚΤΡΑ
μάλιστ᾽ ἐκείνου βοστρύχοις προσείδεται.

ΧΟΡΟΣ
καὶ πῶς ἐκεῖνος δεῦρ᾽ ἐτόλμησεν μολεῖν;

ἨΛΕΚΤΡΑ
ἔπεμψε χαίτην κουρίμην χάριν πατρός.   180

ΧΟΡΟΣ
οὐχ ἧσσον εὐδάκρυτά μοι λέγεις τάδε,
εἰ τῆσδε χώρας μήποτε ψαύσει ποδί.

ἨΛΕΚΤΡΑ
κἀμοὶ προσέστη καρδίας κλυδώνιον
χολῆς, ἐπαίσθην δ᾽ ὡς διανταίῳ βέλει·
ἐξ ὀμμάτων δὲ δίψιοι πίπτουσί μοι   185
σταγόνες ἄφρακτοι δυσχίμου πλημμυρίδος,
πλόκαμον ἰδούσῃ τόνδε· πῶς γὰρ ἐλπίσω
ἀστῶν τιν᾽ ἄλλον τῆσδε δεσπόζειν φόβης;
ἀλλ᾽ οὐδὲ μήν νιν ἡ κτανοῦσ᾽ ἐκείρατο,
ἐμὴ δὲ μήτηρ, οὐδαμῶς ἐπώνυμον   190
φρόνημα παισὶ δύσθεον πεπαμένη.
ἐγὼ δ᾽ ὅπως μὲν ἄντικρυς τάδ᾽ αἰνέσω,
εἶναι τόδ᾽ ἀγλάισμά μοι τοῦ φιλτάτου
βροτῶν Ὀρέστου—σαίνομαι δ᾽ ὑπ᾽ ἐλπίδος.
φεῦ.
εἴθ᾽ εἶχε φωνὴν εὔφρον᾽ ἀγγέλου δίκην,   195

18

ELECTRA

Look at this . . . It looks just like . . .

CHORUS

Like whose?

I want to know.

ELECTRA

Like mine. It looks identical.

CHORUS

Perhaps Orestes? Did he place it here,
a secret offering?

ELECTRA

It really looks like his . . .
these curls . . .

CHORUS

But how could he come back?

ELECTRA

He sent it here, a token of respect   [180]
for his dead father.

CHORUS

Those words of yours
give us fresh cause for tears, if there's no chance
Orestes will set foot in this land again.

ELECTRA

Over my heart, too, breaks a bitter wave.
I feel as if a sword had sliced right through me.
Seeing this hair, my eyes weep thirsty drops—
I can't hold back my flood of grief. There's no way
I would expect one of the citizens,
someone in Argos, to own this lock.
It's clearly not that murderess' hair,
my mother's—her treatment of her children   [190]
profanes the very name of mother.
But how can I accept without a doubt
this offering's from the man I love the most,
Orestes? I'm just clinging to a hope.
Alas! If only, like a messenger,
this hair possessed a friendly human voice,

ὅπως δίφροντις οὖσα μὴ 'κινυσσόμην,
ἀλλ' εὖ 'σαφήνει τόνδ' ἀποπτύσαι πλόκον,
εἴπερ γ' ἀπ' ἐχθροῦ κρατὸς ἦν τετμημένος,
ἢ ξυγγενὴς ὢν εἶχε συμπενθεῖν ἐμοὶ
ἄγαλμα τύμβου τοῦδε καὶ τιμὴν πατρός.   200

ἀλλ' εἰδότας μὲν τοὺς θεοὺς καλούμεθα,
οἵοισιν ἐν χειμῶσι ναυτίλων δίκην
στροβούμεθ'· εἰ δὲ χρὴ τυχεῖν σωτηρίας,
σμικροῦ γένοιτ' ἂν σπέρματος μέγας πυθμήν.

καὶ μὴν στίβοι γε, δεύτερον τεκμήριον,   205
ποδῶν ὅμοιοι τοῖς τ' ἐμοῖσιν ἐμφερεῖς—
καὶ γὰρ δύ' ἐστὸν τώδε περιγραφὰ ποδοῖν,
αὐτοῦ τ' ἐκείνου καὶ συνεμπόρου τινός.
πτέρναι τενόντων θ' ὑπογραφαὶ μετρούμεναι
εἰς ταὐτὸ συμβαίνουσι τοῖς ἐμοῖς στίβοις.   210
πάρεστι δ' ὠδὶς καὶ φρενῶν καταφθορά.

ὈΡΕΣΤΗΣ
εὔχου τὰ λοιπά, τοῖς θεοῖς τελεσφόρους
εὐχὰς ἐπαγγέλλουσα, τυγχάνειν καλῶς.

ἨΛΕΚΤΡΑ
ἐπεὶ τί νῦν ἕκατι δαιμόνων κυρῶ;

ὈΡΕΣΤΗΣ
εἰς ὄψιν ἥκεις ὧνπερ ἐξηύχου πάλαι.   215

ἨΛΕΚΤΡΑ
καὶ τίνα σύνοισθά μοι καλουμένῃ βροτῶν;

ὈΡΕΣΤΗΣ
σύνοιδ' Ὀρέστην πολλά σ' ἐκπαγλουμένην.

ἨΛΕΚΤΡΑ
καὶ πρὸς τί δῆτα τυγχάνω κατευγμάτων;

my thoughts would not be so distracted.
It would tell me clearly what to do.
If someone I detest had cut it off,
I'd throw this lock away, but if it's his,
my brother's, it could share my sorrow,
adorn this tomb, a tribute to my father.   [200]
I call upon the gods who understand
how storms whirl us off course, like sailors.
But if we're fated to come safely home,
then mighty trees can spring from tiny seeds.

[Electra notices footprints in the dirt around the tomb]

Here are some footprints—more evidence—
tracks of feet, just like my own—in pairs—
two sets of footprints, his own and others,
some companion's. The heels, the arches—
these prints are shaped just like my own . . .   [210]

[Electra traces the tracks from the tomb towards Orestes' hiding place. Orestes emerges to meet her as she follows the footprints]

The pain of this . . . my mind grows dizzy . . .

ORESTES
Pray for what must still be done. Thank the gods
for answering your prayers. Pray to them
that all will work out well.

ELECTRA
                                                    What? The gods?
What have they given me?

ORESTES
                                        You've come to see
the person you've been praying for all this time.

ELECTRA
Then you know the man I was calling for?

ORESTES
I know your sympathies are with Orestes.

ELECTRA
Yes, but how have my prayers been answered now?

21

ὈΡΕΣΤΗΣ

ὅδ᾽ εἰμί· μὴ μάτευ᾽ ἐμοῦ μᾶλλον φίλον.

ἩΛΕΚΤΡΑ

ἀλλ᾽ ἦ δόλον τιν᾽, ὦ ξέν᾽, ἀμφί μοι πλέκεις;   220

ὈΡΕΣΤΗΣ

αὐτὸς καθ᾽ αὑτοῦ τἄρα μηχανορραφῶ.

ἩΛΕΚΤΡΑ

ἀλλ᾽ ἐν κακοῖσι τοῖς ἐμοῖς γελᾶν θέλεις.

ὈΡΕΣΤΗΣ

κἂν τοῖς ἐμοῖς ἄρ᾽, εἴπερ ἔν γε τοῖσι σοῖς

ἩΛΕΚΤΡΑ

ὡς ὄντ᾽ Ὀρέστην τάδε σ᾽ ἐγὼ προσεννέπω;

ὈΡΕΣΤΗΣ

αὐτὸν μὲν οὖν ὁρῶσα δυσμαθεῖς ἐμέ·   225
κουρὰν δ᾽ ἰδοῦσα τήνδε κηδείου τριχὸς
ἰχνοσκοποῦσά τ᾽ ἐν στίβοισι τοῖς ἐμοῖς
ἀνεπτερώθης κἀδόκεις ὁρᾶν ἐμέ.
σκέψαι τομῇ προσθεῖσα βόστρυχον τριχὸς
σαυτῆς ἀδελφοῦ σύμμετρον τὠμῷ κάρᾳ.   230
ἰδοῦ δ᾽ ὕφασμα τοῦτο, σῆς ἔργον χερός,
σπάθης τε πληγὰς ἠδὲ θήρειον γραφήν.
ἔνδον γενοῦ, χαρᾷ δὲ μὴ ᾽κπλαγῇς φρένας·
τοὺς φιλτάτους γὰρ οἶδα νῷν ὄντας πικρούς.

ἩΛΕΚΤΡΑ

ὦ φίλτατον μέλημα δώμασιν πατρός,   235
δακρυτὸς ἐλπὶς σπέρματος σωτηρίου,
ἀλκῇ πεποιθὼς δῶμ᾽ ἀνακτήσῃ πατρός.
ὦ τερπνὸν ὄμμα τέσσαρας μοίρας ἔχον

ORESTES

    I'm here. You need look no more for friends.
    I'm the dearest one you have.

ELECTRA

                          No, stranger.
    You're weaving a net, a trick to trap me.   [220]

ORESTES

    If so, I plot against myself as well.

ELECTRA

    You just want to laugh at my distress.

ORESTES

    If I laugh at you, I'm laughing at myself.

ELECTRA

    Orestes . . . is it truly you? Can I
    call you Orestes?

ORESTES

                     Yes, you can.
    You're looking at Orestes in the flesh.
    Why take so long to recognize the truth?
    When you saw the lock of hair, that token
    of my grief, and traced my footprints in the dust,
    your imagination flew—you thought
    you saw me. Look. Put this hair in place.   [230]
    It's your brother's. And it matches yours.
    See this weaving here—that's your handiwork.
    You worked the loom. Look at this design,
    these animals . . .

[Electra is finally convinced. She almost breaks down with joy]

               Control yourself. Calm down.
    Don't get too overjoyed. Remember this—
    our closest family is our enemy.

ELECTRA

    You dearest member of your father's house.
    the seed of hope through all our weeping—
    trust to your own strength and win back again
    your father's home. How my eyes rejoice!
    To me you are four different loves—fate

Aeschylus

ἐμοί· προσαυδᾶν δ' ἐστ' ἀναγκαίως ἔχον
πατέρα τε, καὶ τὸ μητρὸς ἐς σέ μοι ῥέπει   240
στέργηθρον· ἡ δὲ πανδίκως ἐχθαίρεται·
καὶ τῆς τυθείσης νηλεῶς ὁμοσπόρου·
πιστὸς δ' ἀδελφὸς ἦσθ', ἐμοὶ σέβας φέρων
μόνος· Κράτος τε καὶ Δίκη σὺν τῷ τρίτῳ
πάντων μεγίστῳ Ζηνὶ συγγένοιτό σοι.   245

ΟΡΕΣΤΗΣ
Ζεῦ Ζεῦ, θεωρὸς τῶνδε πραγμάτων γενοῦ·
ἰδοῦ δὲ γένναν εὖνιν αἰετοῦ πατρός,
θανόντος ἐν πλεκταῖσι καὶ σπειράμασιν
δεινῆς ἐχίδνης. τοὺς δ' ἀπωρφανισμένους
νῆστις πιέζει λιμός· οὐ γὰρ ἐντελεῖς   250
θήραν πατρῴαν προσφέρειν σκηνήμασιν.
οὕτω δὲ κἀμὲ τήνδε τ', Ἠλέκτραν λέγω,
ἰδεῖν πάρεστί σοι, πατροστερῆ γόνον,
ἄμφω φυγὴν ἔχοντε τὴν αὐτὴν δόμων.
καὶ τοῦ θυτῆρος καί σε τιμῶντος μέγα   255
πατρὸς νεοσσοὺς τούσδ' ἀποφθείρας πόθεν
ἕξεις ὁμοίας χειρὸς εὔθοινον γέρας;
οὔτ' αἰετοῦ γένεθλ' ἀποφθείρας, πάλιν
πέμπειν ἔχοις ἂν σήματ' εὐπιθῆ βροτοῖς·
οὔτ' ἀρχικός σοι πᾶς ὅδ' αὐανθεὶς πυθμὴν   260
βωμοῖς ἀρήξει βουθύτοις ἐν ἤμασιν.
κόμιζ', ἀπὸ σμικροῦ δ' ἂν ἄρειας μέγαν
δόμον, δοκοῦντα κάρτα νῦν πεπτωκέναι.

ΧΟΡΟΣ
ὦ παῖδες, ὦ σωτῆρες ἑστίας πατρός,
σιγᾶθ', ὅπως μὴ πεύσεταί τις, ὦ τέκνα,   265
γλώσσης χάριν δὲ πάντ' ἀπαγγείλῃ τάδε
πρὸς τοὺς κρατοῦντας· οὓς ἴδοιμ' ἐγώ ποτε
θανόντας ἐν κηκῖδι πισσήρει φλογός.

ΟΡΕΣΤΗΣ
οὔτοι προδώσει Λοξίου μεγασθενὴς
χρησμὸς κελεύων τόνδε κίνδυνον περᾶν,   270

24

declares that I must call you father,
and on you falls the love I ought to feel   [240]
towards my mother, who's earned my hate.
Then there's the love I bore my sister,
Iphigeneia, that cruel sacrifice—
and you're my faithful brother. You alone
sustained my sense of honour. May Power
and Justice stand with us now, our allies—
and may almighty Zeus make up the third.

ORESTES

O Zeus, Zeus, look down on what we do!
See the abandoned fledglings of the eagle,
whose father perished in the viper's coils,
that deadly net. Orphans now, we bear
the pangs of hunger, not yet mature enough   [250]
to bring our father's quarry to the nest.
See us like this—I mean me and Electra—
children without a father, both outcasts,
banished from our home. If you wipe out
these fledglings, what respect will you receive
at feasts from hands like his, their father's,
who offered you such wealthy sacrifice?
Kill off the eagle's brood, then who will trust
the signs you send? If this royal stock decays,   [260]
it cannot consecrate your altars
with sacrificial oxen in the morning.
Stand by us. You can elevate our house
from its debased condition, make it great,
though now it seems completely ruined.

CHORUS LEADER

Children, saviours of your father's home,
don't speak too loud. Someone may hear you,
my children, and to hear his tongue run on
report to those in charge. O how I wish
I see them dead one day, roasting in flames,
sizzling like pitch.

ORESTES

                    Apollo's great oracle
surely will defend me. Its orders were
that I should undertake this danger.   [270]

25

Aeschylus

κἀξορθιάζων πολλὰ καὶ δυσχειμέρους
ἄτας ὑφ' ἧπαρ θερμὸν ἐξαυδώμενος,
εἰ μὴ μέτειμι τοῦ πατρὸς τοὺς αἰτίους·
τρόπον τὸν αὐτὸν ἀνταποκτεῖναι λέγων,
ἀποχρημάτοισι ζημίαις ταυρούμενον·   275
αὐτὸν δ' ἔφασκε τῇ φίλῃ ψυχῇ τάδε
τείσειν μ' ἔχοντα πολλὰ δυστερπῆ κακά.
τὰ μὲν γὰρ ἐκ γῆς δυσφρόνων μηνίματα
βροτοῖς πιφαύσκων εἶπε, τὰς δ' αἰνῶν νόσους,
σαρκῶν ἐπαμβατῆρας ἀγρίαις γνάθοις   280
λειχῆνας ἐξέσθοντας ἀρχαίαν φύσιν·
λευκὰς δὲ κόρσας τῇδ' ἐπαντέλλειν νόσῳ·
ἄλλας τ' ἐφώνει προσβολὰς Ἐρινύων
ἐκ τῶν πατρῴων αἱμάτων τελουμένας·
τὸ γὰρ σκοτεινὸν τῶν ἐνερτέρων βέλος   285
ἐκ προστροπαίων ἐν γένει πεπτωκότων,
καὶ λύσσα καὶ μάταιος ἐκ νυκτῶν φόβος
ὁρῶντα λαμπρὸν ἐν σκότῳ νωμῶντ' ὀφρὺν
κινεῖ, ταράσσει, καὶ διώκεσθαι πόλεως
χαλκηλάτῳ πλάστιγγι λυμανθὲν δέμας.   290
καὶ τοῖς τοιούτοις οὔτε κρατῆρος μέρος
εἶναι μετασχεῖν, οὐ φιλοσπόνδου λιβός,
βωμῶν τ' ἀπείργειν οὐχ ὁρωμένην πατρὸς
μῆνιν· δέχεσθαι <δ'> οὔτε συλλύειν τινά.
πάντων δ' ἄτιμον κἄφιλον θνῄσκειν χρόνῳ   295
κακῶς ταριχευθέντα παμφθάρτῳ μόρῳ.
τοιοῖσδε χρησμοῖς ἆρα χρὴ πεποιθέναι;
κεἰ μὴ πέποιθα, τοὔργον ἔστ' ἐργαστέον.
πολλοὶ γὰρ εἰς ἓν συμπίτνουσιν ἵμεροι,
θεοῦ τ' ἐφετμαὶ καὶ πατρὸς πένθος μέγα,   300
καὶ πρὸς πιέζει χρημάτων ἀχηνία,
τὸ μὴ πολίτας εὐκλεεστάτους βροτῶν,
Τροίας ἀναστατῆρας εὐδόξῳ φρενί,
δυοῖν γυναικοῖν ὧδ' ὑπηκόους πέλειν.
θήλεια γὰρ φρήν· εἰ δὲ μή, τάχ' εἴσεται.   305

26

It cried out in prophecy, foretelling
many winters of calamity would chill
my hot heart, if I did not take revenge
on those who killed my father. It ordered me
to murder them the way they murdered him,
insisting they could not pay the penalty
with their possessions. The oracle declared,
"If not, you'll pay the debt with your own life,
a life of troubles." It spoke a revelation,
making known to men the wrath of blood guilt—
from underneath the earth, infectious plagues,
leprous sores which gnaw the flesh, fangs chewing   [280]
living tissue, festering white rot in the sores.
It mentioned other miseries as well—
attacks by vengeful Furies, stemming
from a slaughtered father's blood, dark bolts
from gods below, aroused by murdered kinsmen
calling for revenge, frenzied night fits.[3]
Such terrors plague the man—he sees them all
so clearly, eyeballs rolling in the dark.
Then he's chased in exile from the city,
his body scourged by bronze-tipped whips.   [290]
A man like this can never share the wine bowl,
no libations mixed with love. We don't see
his father's anger, but it casts him out—
no access to an altar. There's no relief,
and no one takes him in, until at last,
universally despised, without a friend,
he wastes in all-consuming pain and dies.
Am I not right to trust such oracles?
Even if I don't, the work must still be done.
Many feelings lead to one conclusion—
the gods' decree, my keen paternal grief,   [300]
the weight of poverty I bear. Besides,
my countrymen, most glorious of men,
whose courageous spirit brought down Troy,
should not be subject to a pair of women.
For Aegisthus is at heart a woman—
if not, we'll learn about it soon enough.

Aeschylus

ΧΟΡΟΣ
ἀλλ' ὦ μεγάλαι Μοῖραι, Διόθεν
τῆδε τελευτᾶν,
τὸ δίκαιον μεταβαίνει.
ἀντὶ μὲν ἐχθρᾶς γλώσσης ἐχθρὰ
γλῶσσα τελείσθω· τοὐφειλόμενον   310
πράσσουσα Δίκη μέγ' αὐτεῖ·
'ἀντὶ δὲ πληγῆς φονίας φονίαν
πληγὴν τινέτω. δράσαντι παθεῖν,'
τριγέρων μῦθος τάδε φωνεῖ.

ΟΡΕΣΤΗΣ
ὦ πάτερ αἰνόπατερ, τί σοι   315
φάμενος ἢ τί ῥέξας
τύχοιμ' ἂν ἔκαθεν οὐρίσας,
ἔνθα σ' ἔχουσιν εὐναί,
σκότῳ φάος ἀντίμοι-
ρον; χάριτες δ' ὁμοίως   320
κέκληνται γόος εὐκλεὴς
προσθοδόμοις Ἀτρείδαις.

ΧΟΡΟΣ
τέκνον, φρόνημα τοῦ
θανόντος οὐ δαμάζει
πυρὸς [ἡ] μαλερὰ γνάθος,   325
φαίνει δ' ὕστερον ὀργάς·
ὀτοτύζεται δ' ὁ θνῄσκων,
ἀναφαίνεται δ' ὁ βλάπτων.
πατέρων τε καὶ τεκόντων
γόος ἔνδικος ματεύει   330
τὸ πᾶν ἀμφιλαφής ταραχθείς.

ΗΛΕΚΤΡΑ
κλῦθὶ νυν, ὦ πάτερ, ἐν μέρει
πολυδάκρυτα πένθη.
δίπαις τοί σ' ἐπιτύμβιος
θρῆνος ἀναστενάζει.   335
τάφος δ' ἱκέτας δέδεκται
φυγάδας θ' ὁμοίως.

28

CHORUS

Oh mighty Fates, bring all this to pass.
Through Zeus' power, make all things right.
For Justice, as she turns the scales
exacting retribution, cries aloud,
"Hostile words for hostile words—   [310]
let it be done. One murderous stroke
is paid off by another lethal blow.
The one who acts must suffer."
So runs the ancient saying,
now three generations old.

ORESTES

O my unhappy father,
what can I say for you or do,
to send you, where you rest
so far away, some light
to drive away your darkness?
But nonetheless some joy   [320]
comes from a funeral lament
for glorious sons of Atreus,
who once possessed the house.[4]

CHORUS

My child, among the dead
the savage jaws of fire
cannot destroy the spirit.
He'll show his rage in time.
Dead men receive their dirge—
the guilty stand revealed.
A father's funeral lament,
strong and clear and just,
searches far and wide,   [330]
confounding those who killed.

ELECTRA

Hear us now, my father,
as, in turn, we mourn and weep.
Your two children at your tomb
now sing your death song.
Your tomb has welcomed us,
two suppliants and outcasts.

Aeschylus

τί τῶνδ' εὖ, τί δ' ἄτερ κακῶν;
οὐκ ἀτρίακτος ἄτα;

ΧΟΡΟΣ

ἀλλ' ἔτ' ἂν ἐκ τῶνδε θεὸς χρῄζων   340
θείη κελάδους εὐφθογγοτέρους·
ἀντὶ δὲ θρήνων ἐπιτυμβιδίων
παιὰν μελάθροις ἐν βασιλείοις
νεοκρᾶτα φίλον κομίσειεν.

ΟΡΕΣΤΗΣ

εἰ γὰρ ὑπ' Ἰλίῳ   345
πρός τινος Λυκίων, πάτερ,
δορίτμητος κατηναρίσθης·
λιπὼν ἂν εὔκλειαν ἐν δόμοισι
τέκνων τ' ἐν κελεύθοις
ἐπιστρεπτὸν αἰῶ   350
κτίσας πολύχωστον ἂν εἶχες
τάφον διαποντίου γᾶς
δώμασιν εὐφόρητον,

ΧΟΡΟΣ

φίλος φίλοισι τοῖς
ἐκεῖ καλῶς θανοῦσιν   355
κατὰ χθονὸς ἐμπρέπων
σεμνότιμος ἀνάκτωρ,
πρόπολός τε τῶν μεγίστων
χθονίων ἐκεῖ τυράννων·
βασιλεὺς γὰρ ἦσθ', ὄφρ' ἔζης,   360
μόριμον λάχος πιπλάντων
χεροῖν πεισίβροτόν τε βάκτρον.

ΗΛΕΚΤΡΑ

μηδ' ὑπὸ Τρωίας
τείχεσι φθίμενος, πάτερ,
μετ' ἄλλῳ δουρικμῆτι λαῷ   365
παρὰ Σκαμάνδρου πόρον τεθάφθαι.

30

What in this is good?
What free from trouble?
Who wrestles death and wins?

CHORUS
But if god wills it, he can turn   [340]
our dirges into joyful songs—
instead of funeral laments
around this monument
chants of triumph ringing out
throughout the palace halls,
a welcome celebration
for reunion with a friend.

ORESTES
My father, if only you had died
hit by some Lycian spear at Troy!
You'd have left your glory
with your children in their home.
In their dealings with the world
men would now honour them.   [350]
You'd have won a tomb raised high
in lands across the seas, a death
your home could bear with ease.

CHORUS
Dear to the men you loved,
the ones who died so bravely,
you'd stand out under earth,
as a majestic lord, minister
of the mightiest gods below,
who rule the dead. In life,
you were a king of men—   [360]
the ones who hold the staff
that every man obeys,
those with authority
to sentence men to die.

ELECTRA
I don't want you dead, my father,
not even under Trojan walls,
with all those other men
who perished by the spear,
where the Scamander flows.5

πάρος δ' οἱ κτανόντες
νιν οὕτως δαμῆναι
⟨φίλοις⟩, θανατηφόρον αἶσαν
πρόσω τινὰ πυνθάνεσθαι   370
τῶνδε πόνων ἄπειρον.

ΧΟΡΟΣ

ταῦτα μέν, ὦ παῖ, κρείσσονα χρυσοῦ,
μεγάλης δὲ τύχης καὶ ὑπερβορέου
μείζονα φωνεῖς· δύνασαι γάρ.
ἀλλὰ διπλῆς γὰρ τῆσδε μαράγνης   375
δοῦπος ἱκνεῖται· τῶν μὲν ἀρωγοὶ
κατὰ γῆς ἤδη, τῶν δὲ κρατούντων
χέρες οὐχ ὅσιαι στυγερῶν τούτων·
παισὶ δὲ μᾶλλον γεγένηται.

ΟΡΕΣΤΗΣ

τοῦτο διαμπερὲς οὖς   380
ἵκεθ' ἅπερ τι βέλος.
Ζεῦ Ζεῦ, κάτωθεν ἀμπέμπων
ὑστερόποινον ἄταν
βροτῶν τλάμονι καὶ πανούργῳ
χειρί—τοκεῦσι δ' ὅμως τελεῖται.

ΧΟΡΟΣ

ἐφυμνῆσαι γένοιτό μοι πυκά-   385
εντ' ὀλολυγμὸν ἀνδρὸς
θεινομένου, γυναικός τ'
ὀλλυμένας· τί γὰρ κεύθω φρενὸς οἷον ἔμπας
ποτᾶται; πάροιθεν δὲ πρώρας   390
δριμὺς ἄηται κραδίας
θυμὸς ἔγκοτον στύγος.

No. I'd much prefer
your killers had been killed
by their own families,
just as they murdered you.
People then in far-off lands
would hear about their deaths   [370]
and not our present trouble.

CHORUS

Children, these things you say
are merely your desires,
finer than gold, greater still
than the great happiness
of those who live in bliss
beyond the northern wind.
But wishing is an easy thing.
Still, now it's striking home,
that double whip—for now
protectors underneath the earth
are helping us. Our masters
are unholy creatures
with polluted hands.
The children win the day!

ORESTES

Our words, like arrows,   [380]
pierce down into the earth
straight to my father's ear.
O Zeus, Zeus, send us
from the world below
your long-delayed revenge,
pay back the wickedness
brought on by human hands.
O let that come to pass—
and thus avenge all fathers.

CHORUS

Let my heart cry out in triumph
when that man is stabbed,
when that woman dies.
Why should my spirit hide
what hovers here before me,
when driving hatred, like a storm,   [390]
a biting headwind,
breaks across my heart?

33

ἨΛΕΚΤΡΑ

καί πότ' ἂν ἀμφιθαλὴς
Ζεὺς ἐπὶ χεῖρα βάλοι,⁣   395
φεῦ φεῦ, κάρανα δαΐξας;
πιστὰ γένοιτο χώρᾳ.
δίκαν δ' ἐξ ἀδίκων ἀπαιτῶ.
κλῦτε δὲ Γᾶ χθονίων τε τιμαί.

ΧΟΡΟΣ

ἀλλὰ νόμος μὲν φονίας σταγόνας⁣   400
χυμένας ἐς πέδον ἄλλο προσαιτεῖν
αἷμα. βοᾷ γὰρ λοιγὸς Ἐρινὺν
παρὰ τῶν πρότερον φθιμένων ἄτην
ἑτέραν ἐπάγουσαν ἐπ' ἄτῃ.

ὈΡΕΣΤΗΣ

πόποι δὴ νερτέρων τυραννίδες,⁣   405
ἴδετε πολυκρατεῖς Ἀραὶ φθινομένων,
ἴδεσθ' Ἀτρειδᾶν τὰ λοίπ' ἀμηχάνως
ἔχοντα καὶ δωμάτων
ἄτιμα. πᾷ τις τράποιτ' ἄν, ὦ Ζεῦ;

ΧΟΡΟΣ

πέπαλται δαῦτέ μοι φίλον κέαρ⁣   410
τόνδε κλύουσαν οἶκτον
καὶ τότε μὲν δύσελπις,
σπλάγχνα δέ μοι κελαινοῦ-
ται πρὸς ἔπος κλυούσᾳ.
ὅταν δ' αὖτ' ἐπ' ἀλκῆς ἐπάρῃ <μ'⁣   415
ἐλπὶς>, ἀπέστασεν ἄχος
προσφανεῖσά μοι καλῶς.

ἨΛΕΚΤΡΑ

τί δ' ἂν φάντες τύχοιμεν ἢ τά περ
πάθομεν ἄχεα πρός γε τῶν τεκομένων;
πάρεστι σαίνειν, τὰ δ' οὔτι θέλγεται.⁣   420
λύκος γὰρ ὥστ' ὠμόφρων
ἄσαντος ἐκ ματρός ἐστι θυμός.

ELECTRA
Oh, when will mighty Zeus
strike them with his fist—
split their skulls apart!
Alas, alas! Give our land
some sign—confirm our faith.
From these crimes I seek
the rights of justice.
O Earth, hear me, and you,
blessed gods in earth below.

CHORUS
It's the law—once drops of blood   [400]
are shed upon the ground
they cry out for still more blood.
Slaughter calls upon the Furies
of those who have been killed.
Thus, hard on murder's heels
destruction comes again.

ORESTES
Lords of the world below, alas,
see the mighty curses of the dead.
See survivors of the line of Atreus,
here in our helplessness,
cast out from home, dishonoured.
O Zeus, where can we turn?

CHORUS
My fond heart races once again   [410]
to hear your pitiful lament.
But as I listen to your words
I lose my hope. My heart
grows dark. But then again
hope comes to make me strong—
all my unhappiness is gone.
I see a bright new dawn.

ELECTRA
To what can we appeal? What else
but to the agonies we suffer,
anguish from the one who bore us,
our mother. So let her grovel.   [420]
She'll not appease our pain.
We're bred from her, like wolves,
whose savage hearts do not relent.

35

Aeschylus

ΧΟΡΟΣ
ἔκοψα κομμὸν Ἄριον ἔν τε Κισσίας
νόμοις ἰηλεμιστρίας,
ἀπριγδόπληκτα πολυπλάνητα δ' ἦν ἰδεῖν 425
ἐπασσυτεροτριβῆ τὰ χερὸς ὀρέγματα
ἄνωθεν ἀνέκαθεν, κτύπῳ δ' ἐπερρόθει
κροτητὸν ἀμὸν καὶ πανάθλιον κάρα.

ἩΛΕΚΤΡΑ
ἰὼ [ἰὼ] δαῖα
πάντολμε μᾶτερ, δαΐαις ἐν ἐκφοραῖς 430
ἄνευ πολιτᾶν ἄνακτ',
ἄνευ δὲ πενθημάτων
ἔτλας ἀνοίμωκτον ἄνδρα θάψαι.

ὈΡΕΣΤΗΣ
τὸ πᾶν ἀτίμως ἔλεξας, οἴμοι.
πατρὸς δ' ἀτίμωσιν ἆρα τείσει 435
ἕκατι μὲν δαιμόνων,
ἕκατι δ' ἀμᾶν χερῶν;
ἔπειτ' ἐγὼ νοσφίσας ὀλοίμαν.

ΧΟΡΟΣ
ἐμασχαλίσθη δέ γ', ὡς τόδ' εἰδῇς·
ἔπρασσε δ', πέρ νιν ὧδε θάπτει, 440
μόρον κτίσαι μωμένα
ἄφερτον αἰῶνι σῷ.
κλύεις πατρῴους δύας ἀτίμους.

ἩΛΕΚΤΡΑ
λέγεις πατρῷον μόρον· ἐγὼ δ' ἀπεστάτουν 445
ἄτιμος, οὐδὲν ἀξία·
μυχῷ δ' ἄφερκτος πολυσινοῦς κυνὸς δίκαν
ἑτοιμότερα γέλωτος ἀνέφερον λίβη,
χέουσα πολύδακρυν γόον κεκρυμμένα.
τοιαῦτ' ἀκούων ἐν φρεσὶν γράφου ⟨◡ -⟩. 450

36

CHORUS

    Like some Asian wailing woman,
    I beat out my lament, my fists
    keep pounding out the blows
    in quick succession. You see
    my hands—I stretch them out,
    then strike down from above.
    My torment beats upon my head
    until it breaks for sorrow.

ELECTRA

    Oh cruel and reckless mother,   [430]
    that savage burial, our king,
    no fellow citizens around,
    no suffering procession—
    you dared place him in the tomb
    without the rites of mourning.

ORESTES

    Alas. As you say, totally disgraced.
    But she'll pay for his dishonour,
    by the gods, by my own hands.
    Let me kill her. Then let me die.

CHORUS

    And let me tell you this—
    she first hacked off his limbs,   [440]
    then hung them round his neck.
    That's how she buried him,
    to make that slaughter
    a burden on your life—
    a thing you couldn't bear.
    You hear me? Your father's death—
    she made it an abomination.

ELECTRA

    You describe my father's death,
    but I too was utterly disgraced,
    worth nothing, set apart,
    inside a cell, as if I were
    some rabid dog. I wept.
    What had I to laugh about,
    as I shed all those tears in hiding?
    Hear that. Carve that on your heart.   [450]

ΧΟΡΟΣ

δι' ὤτων δὲ συν-
τέτραινε μῦθον ἡσύχῳ φρενῶν βάσει.
τὰ μὲν γὰρ οὕτως ἔχει,
τὰ δ' αὐτὸς ὄργα μαθεῖν.
πρέπει δ' ἀκάμπτῳ μένει καθήκειν.   455

ὈΡΕΣΤΗΣ

σὲ τοι λέγω, ξυγγενοῦ, πάτερ, φίλοις.

ἨΛΕΚΤΡΑ

ἐγὼ δ' ἐπιφθέγγομαι κεκλαυμένα.

ΧΟΡΟΣ

στάσις δὲ πάγκοινος ἅδ' ἐπιρροθεῖ·
ἄκουσον ἐς φάος μολών,
ξὺν δὲ γενοῦ πρὸς ἐχθρούς.   460

ὈΡΕΣΤΗΣ

Ἄρης Ἄρει ξυμβαλεῖ, Δίκᾳ Δίκα.

ἨΛΕΚΤΡΑ

ἰὼ θεοί, κραίνετ' ἐνδίκως <δίκας.>

ΧΟΡΟΣ

τρόμος μ' ὑφέρπει κλύουσαν εὐγμάτων.
τὸ μόρσιμον μένει πάλαι,
εὐχομένοις δ' ἂν ἔλθοι.   465

ὦ πόνος ἐγγενὴς
καὶ παράμουσος Ἄτας
αἱματόεσσα πλαγά.
ἰὼ δύστον' ἄφερτα κήδη·
ἰὼ δυσκατάπαυστον ἄλγος.   470

δώμασιν ἔμμοτον
τῶνδ' ἄκος, οὐδ' ἀπ' ἄλλων
ἔκτοθεν, ἀλλ' ἀπ' αὐτῶν,
δι' ὠμὰν ἔριν αἱματηράν.
θεῶν <τῶν> κατὰ γᾶς ὅδ' ὕμνος.   475

CHORUS

    Let your ears pick up her story,
    but keep your spirit firm.
    Things now stand as they stand.
    You're keen to know what's next,
    but you must wait, prepared
    to fight on with no turning back.

ORESTES

    Father, I call on you. Stand by your children.

ELECTRA

    Through these tears I join his call.

CHORUS

    In unison, our voices blend as one—
    hear us. Return into the light.
    Join us against our enemies.   [460]

ORESTES

    Now war god Ares goes to meet
    the war god Ares. Right fights with right.

ELECTRA

    Dear gods, let justice choose what's right.

CHORUS

    I hear these prayers and shudder.
    This doom's been long delayed,
    but it does come for those who pray.

    Oh, family bred for torments,
    for the bloody strokes
    of harsh discordant ruin,
    for pains beyond enduring,
    grief that can't be staunched.   [470]

    For all this evil there's a remedy,
    not from some stranger,
    someone outside the house,
    but from within, the cure
    that blood strife brings,
    their savage bloody fight.
    To gods beneath the ground
    we sing this hymn.

ἀλλὰ κλύοντες, μάκαρες χθόνιοι,
τῆσδε κατευχῆς πέμπετ᾽ ἀρωγὴν
παισὶν προφρόνως ἐπὶ νίκῃ.

ὈΡΕΣΤΗΣ

πάτερ, τρόποισιν οὐ τυραννικοῖς θανών,
αἰτουμένῳ μοι δὸς κράτος τῶν σῶν δόμων.   480

ἨΛΕΚΤΡΑ

κἀγώ, πάτερ, τοιάνδε σου χρείαν ἔχω,
φυγεῖν μέγαν προσθεῖσαν Αἰγίσθῳ ⟨φθόρον⟩.

ὈΡΕΣΤΗΣ

οὕτω γὰρ ἄν σοι δαῖτες ἔννομοι βροτῶν
κτιζοίατ᾽· εἰ δὲ μή, παρ᾽ εὐδείπνοις ἔσῃ
ἄτιμος ἐμπύροισι κνισωτοῖς χθονός.   485

ἨΛΕΚΤΡΑ

κἀγὼ χοάς σοι τῆς ἐμῆς παγκληρίας
οἴσω πατρῴων ἐκ δόμων γαμηλίους·
πάντων δὲ πρῶτον τόνδε πρεσβεύσω τάφον.

ὈΡΕΣΤΗΣ

ὦ Γαῖ, ἄνες μοι πατέρ᾽ ἐποπτεῦσαι μάχην.

ἨΛΕΚΤΡΑ

ὦ Περσέφασσα, δὸς δ᾽ ἔτ᾽ εὔμορφον κράτος.   490

ὈΡΕΣΤΗΣ

μέμνησο λουτρῶν οἷς ἐνοσφίσθης, πάτερ.

ἨΛΕΚΤΡΑ

μέμνησο δ᾽ ἀμφίβληστρον ὡς ἐκαίνισαν.

Hear us, you blessed gods of earth,
hear this supplication, and assist
with your good will these children.
Give them the victory!

ORESTES

Father, you may not have perished like a king,
but, in answer to my prayer, make me   [480]
the master of your house.

ELECTRA

                                I, too, father,
have a request of you—let me escape,
once I've accomplished this enormous task,
once Aegisthus is destroyed.

ORESTES

                                Yes.
Then men would set up on your behalf
those feasts of honour our laws demand.
But otherwise, when people sacrifice
burnt offering to Earth at solemn banquets
they will not honour you.

ELECTRA

                        And I, too,
at my marriage feast, from the full store
of what I inherit in my father's house,
will pour libations to you. And your tomb
I'll honour above all other shrines.

ORESTES

O Earth, send my father up to see our fight.

ELECTRA

O Persephone, grant us glorious power.[6]   [490]

ORESTES

My father, remember that bath
where you were slaughtered.

ELECTRA

Remember the net in which they killed you.

ὈΡΕΣΤΗΣ

πέδαις δ' ἀχαλκεύτοις ἐθηρεύθης, πάτερ.

ἨΛΕΚΤΡΑ

αἰσχρῶς τε βουλευτοῖσιν ἐν καλύμμασιν.

ὈΡΕΣΤΗΣ

ἆρ' ἐξεγείρῃ τοῖσδ' ὀνείδεσιν, πάτερ;   495

ἨΛΕΚΤΡΑ

ἆρ' ὀρθὸν αἴρεις φίλτατον τὸ σὸν κάρα;

ὈΡΕΣΤΗΣ

ἤτοι δίκην ἴαλλε σύμμαχον φίλοις,
ἢ τὰς ὁμοίας ἀντίδος λαβὰς λαβεῖν,
εἴπερ κρατηθείς γ' ἀντινικῆσαι θέλεις.

ἨΛΕΚΤΡΑ

καὶ τῆσδ' ἄκουσον λοισθίου βοῆς, πάτερ,   500
ἰδὼν νεοσσοὺς τούσδ' ἐφημένους τάφῳ·
οἴκτιρε θῆλυν ἄρσενός θ' ὁμοῦ γόνον.

ὈΡΕΣΤΗΣ

καὶ μὴ 'ξαλείψῃς σπέρμα Πελοπιδῶν τόδε·
οὕτω γὰρ οὐ τέθνηκας οὐδὲ περ θανών·

ἨΛΕΚΤΡΑ

παῖδες γὰρ ἀνδρὶ κληδόνες σωτήριοι   505
θανόντι· φελλοὶ δ' ὡς ἄγουσι δίκτυον,
τὸν ἐκ βυθοῦ κλωστῆρα σῴζοντες λίνου.

ὈΡΕΣΤΗΣ

ἄκου', ὑπὲρ σοῦ τοιάδ' ἔστ' ὀδύρματα.
αὐτὸς δὲ σῴζῃ τόνδε τιμήσας λόγον.

ΧΟΡΟΣ

καὶ μὴν ἀμεμφῆ τόνδ' ἐτείνατον λόγον,   510
τίμημα τύμβου τῆς ἀνοιμώκτου τύχης.

ORESTES

My father, you were trapped in fetters,
but they weren't forged in bronze.

ELECTRA

They covered you
with their deceit and shame.

ORESTES

Father, these taunts—
do they not stir your spirit?

ELECTRA

Will you raise
that beloved head of yours upright?

ORESTES

Either send Justice here to stand with us,
the ones you love, or let us, in our turn,
catch them in our grip, as they caught you—
that is, if you want to beat them down,
after the way they overpowered you.

ELECTRA

Father, listen to my last appeal—   [500]
see your children huddled at your tomb.
Take pity on them, your son and daughter.

ORESTES

Don't let the seed of Pelops disappear.
With us alive, in death you cannot die.7

ELECTRA

For to a man that's dead his children
are saving testament—like corks,
they hold up the net and keep the mesh
from sinking deep into the sea.

ORESTES

Hear us!
We're making our lament on your behalf.
Honour our request and save yourself.

CHORUS LEADER

There's nothing wrong expanding your lament.   [510]
For that will honour this neglected tomb.

43

τὰ δ’ ἄλλ’, ἐπειδὴ δρᾶν κατώρθωσαι φρενί,
ἔρδοις ἂν ἤδη δαίμονος πειρώμενος.

ὈΡΕΣΤΗΣ

ἔσται· πυθέσθαι δ’ οὐδέν ἐστ’ ἔξω δρόμου,
πόθεν χοὰς ἔπεμψεν, ἐκ τίνος λόγου   515
μεθύστερον τιμῶσ’ ἀνήκεστον πάθος;
θανόντι δ’ οὐ φρονοῦντι δειλαία χάρις
ἐπέμπετ’· οὐκ ἔχοιμ’ ἂν εἰκάσαι τόδε.
τὰ δῶρα μείω δ’ ἐστὶ τῆς ἁμαρτίας.
τὰ πάντα γάρ τις ἐκχέας ἀνθ’ αἵματος   520
ἑνός, μάτην ὁ μόχθος· ὧδ’ ἔχει λόγος.
θέλοντι δ’, εἴπερ οἶσθ’, ἐμοὶ φράσον τάδε.

ΧΟΡΟΣ

οἶδ’, ὦ τέκνον, παρῆ γάρ· ἔκ τ’ ὀνειράτων
καὶ νυκτιπλάγκτων δειμάτων πεπαλμένη
χοὰς ἔπεμψε τάσδε δύσθεος γυνή.   525

ὈΡΕΣΤΗΣ

ἦ καὶ πέπυσθε τοὔναρ, ὥστ’ ὀρθῶς φράσαι;

ΧΟΡΟΣ

τεκεῖν δράκοντ’ ἔδοξεν, ὡς αὐτὴ λέγει.

ὈΡΕΣΤΗΣ

καὶ ποῖ τελευτᾷ καὶ καρανοῦται λόγος;

ΧΟΡΟΣ

ἐν σπαργάνοισι παιδὸς ὁρμίσαι δίκην.

ὈΡΕΣΤΗΣ

τίνος βορᾶς χρῄζοντα, νεογενὲς δάκος;   530

ΧΟΡΟΣ

αὐτὴ προσέσχε μαζὸν ἐν τὠνείρατι.

ὈΡΕΣΤΗΣ

καὶ πῶς ἄτρωτον οὖθαρ ἦν ὑπὸ στύγους;

But since your heart is rightly set to act,
it's time to test your fortune, time to start.

ORESTES

You're right. But first we might ask this question:
Why did that woman send out these libations?
What did she have in mind, trying so late
to heal a crime which cannot be forgiven?
What she sent here was paltry tribute
to the unforgiving dead. I don't see
what she intends. The gift's too trivial
for her offence. As the old saying runs,
"Pour out all you've got to make amends   [520]
for bloodshed, your work is all in vain."
If you know her reason, tell me now.
I'd like to hear.

CHORUS LEADER

              My child, I know—I was there.
She had bad dreams. Vague terrors in the night
upset her. So that godless woman sent these gifts.

ORESTES

Do you know the nature of her dreams?
Can you give me details?

CHORUS LEADER

                   She'd given birth,
but to a snake. That's what she told me.

ORESTES

How did the dream end up? What happened?

CHORUS LEADER

She set it in bed wrapped in swaddling clothes,
just like a child.

ORESTES

            And that newborn snake,
what did it want for nourishment?   [530]

CHORUS LEADER

She dreamt she offered it her breasts.

ORESTES

Didn't the monster bite her nipple?

ΧΟΡΟΣ

ὥστ᾽ ἐν γάλακτι θρόμβον αἵματος σπάσαι.

ΟΡΕΣΤΗΣ

οὔτοι μάταιον· ἀνδρὸς ὄψανον πέλει.

ΧΟΡΟΣ

ἡ δ᾽ ἐξ ὕπνου κέκλαγγεν ἐπτοημένη.   535
πολλοὶ δ᾽ ἀνῆθον, ἐκτυφλωθέντες σκότῳ,
λαμπτῆρες ἐν δόμοισι δεσποίνης χάριν·
πέμπει τ᾽ ἔπειτα τάσδε κηδείους χοάς,
ἄκος τομαῖον ἐλπίσασα πημάτων.

ΟΡΕΣΤΗΣ

ἀλλ᾽ εὔχομαι γῇ τῇδε καὶ πατρὸς τάφῳ   540
τοὔνειρον εἶναι τοῦτ᾽ ἐμοὶ τελεσφόρον.
κρίνω δέ τοί νιν ὥστε συγκόλλως ἔχειν.
εἰ γὰρ τὸν αὐτὸν χῶρον ἐκλιπὼν ἐμοὶ
οὔφις ἐμοῖσι σπαργάνοις ὡπλίζετο,
καὶ μαστὸν ἀμφέχασκ᾽ ἐμὸν θρεπτήριον,   545
θρόμβῳ δ᾽ ἔμειξεν αἵματος φίλον γάλα,
ἡ δ᾽ ἀμφὶ τάρβει τῷδ᾽ ἐπώμωξεν πάθει,
δεῖ τοί νιν, ὡς ἔθρεψεν ἔκπαγλον τέρας,
θανεῖν βιαίως· ἐκδρακοντωθεὶς δ᾽ ἐγὼ
κτείνω νιν, ὡς τοὔνειρον ἐννέπει τόδε.   550

ΧΟΡΟΣ

τερασκόπον δὴ τῶνδέ σ᾽ αἱροῦμαι πέρι.
γένοιτο δ᾽ οὕτως. τἄλλα δ᾽ ἐξηγοῦ φίλοις,
τοὺς μέν τι ποιεῖν, τοὺς δὲ μή τι δρᾶν λέγων.

ΟΡΕΣΤΗΣ

ἁπλοῦς ὁ μῦθος· τήνδε μὲν στείχειν ἔσω,
αἰνῶ δὲ κρύπτειν τάσδε συνθήκας ἐμάς,   555
ὡς ἂν δόλῳ κτείναντες ἄνδρα τίμιον
δόλοισι καὶ ληφθῶσιν ἐν ταὐτῷ βρόχῳ
θανόντες, καὶ Λοξίας ἐφήμισεν,
ἄναξ Ἀπόλλων, μάντις ἀψευδὴς τὸ πρίν.

CHORUS LEADER

No. But with her milk it sucked out clots of blood.

ORESTES

It's an omen. Her vision means a man.

CHORUS LEADER

She woke up with a scream, quite terrified.
Many torches which stay unlit at night
were set ablaze throughout the house
to calm our mistress. Then she sent out
libations for the dead—in the hope
they'd work like medicine for her distress.

ORESTES

I pray to Earth and to my father's tomb   [540]
that this dream will fulfill itself in me.
I think it matches me in every point.
If that snake came from the same womb as me,
if it was wrapped up in my swaddling clothes
and opened up its jaws to suck the milk
that nourished me, mixing sweet milk with blood,
so she cried out in terror at the sight,
then that must mean she'll die by violence,
from nursing such a violent beast.
I am that snake. And I will kill her.   [550]
That's the meaning of this dream.

CHORUS LEADER

Your reading of her dream seems right to me.
So let it come. Tell your friends the rest—
what they must do or take care not to do.

ORESTES

My plan is simple. First, Electra here
must go inside. I'm instructing her
to keep this bond with me a secret.
The two in there deceived a noble man,
then killed him. So we'll use deceit on them.
They'll die in the same net. Lord Apollo,
who's never wrong in what he prophesies,

47

ξένῳ γὰρ εἰκώς, παντελῆ σαγὴν ἔχων,   560
ἥξω σὺν ἀνδρὶ τῷδ᾽ ἐφ᾽ ἑρκείους πύλας
Πυλάδῃ, ξένος τε καὶ δορύξενος δόμων.
ἄμφω δὲ φωνὴν ἥσομεν Παρνησσίδα,
γλώσσης αὐτὴν Φωκίδος μιμουμένω.
καὶ δὴ θυρωρῶν οὔτις ἂν φαιδρᾷ φρενὶ   565
δέξαιτ᾽, ἐπειδὴ δαιμονᾷ δόμος κακοῖς·
μενοῦμεν οὕτως ὥστ᾽ ἐπεικάζειν τινὰ
δόμους παραστείχοντα καὶ τάδ᾽ ἐννέπειν·
'τί δὴ πύλαισι τὸν ἱκέτην ἀπείργεται
Αἴγισθος, εἴπερ οἶδεν ἔνδημος παρών;'   570
εἰ δ᾽ οὖν ἀμείψω βαλὸν ἑρκείων πυλῶν
κἀκεῖνον ἐν θρόνοισιν εὑρήσω πατρός,
ἢ καὶ μολὼν ἔπειτά μοι κατὰ στόμα
ἀρεῖ, σάφ᾽ ἴσθι, καὶ κατ᾽ ὀφθαλμοὺς βαλεῖ,
πρὶν αὐτὸν εἰπεῖν 'ποδαπὸς ὁ ξένος;' νεκρὸν   575
θήσω, ποδώκει περιβαλὼν χαλκεύματι.
φόνου δ᾽ Ἐρινὺς οὐχ ὑπεσπανισμένη
ἄκρατον αἷμα πίεται τρίτην πόσιν.
νῦν οὖν σὺ μὲν φύλασσε τἀν οἴκῳ καλῶς,
ὅπως ἂν ἀρτίκολλα συμβαίνῃ τάδε·   580
ὑμῖν δ᾽ ἐπαινῶ γλῶσσαν εὔφημον φέρειν,
σιγᾶν θ᾽ ὅπου δεῖ καὶ λέγειν τὰ καίρια.
τὰ δ᾽ ἄλλα τούτῳ δεῦρ᾽ ἐποπτεῦσαι λέγω,
ξιφηφόρους ἀγῶνας ὀρθώσαντί μοι.

ΧΟΡΟΣ
    πολλὰ μὲν γᾶ τρέφει   585
    δεινὰ [καὶ] δειμάτων ἄχη,
    πόντιαί τ᾽ ἀγκάλαι κνωδάλων
    ἀνταίων βρύουσι·
    πλάθουσι [βλαστοῦσι] καὶ πεδαίχμιοι
    λαμπάδες πεδάοροι,   590
    πτανά τε καὶ πεδοβά-
    μονα κἀνεμόεντ᾽ ἂν
    αἰγίδων φράσαι κότον.

has ordered this. I'll approach the outer gates,   [560]
pretending I'm a stranger, prepared
for anything. Pylades goes with me,
as guest and ally of the house. We two
will speak Parnassian dialect of Phocis.
If no one at the gate is in the mood
to let us in, alleging that the house
is haunted by some evil demon,
we'll wait there so any passer-by
will be intrigued and say, "What's going on?
Why does Aegisthus shut his doors like this   [570]
against a suppliant? Is he at home?
Is he aware of this?" If I get past the gate,
across the outer threshold, then find that man
seated on my father's throne or meet him
face to face, his eyes will shift and fall,
I promise you. Before he's had time to ask,
"Stranger, what country are you from?"
I'll kill him quickly with my sword.
Our Fury never lacked for blood—
for her third draught she'll drink his pure.
Now, Electra, keep a close watch in there,
check what's going on inside the house.
We'll need to work on this together.   [580]
You women, be careful what you say—
keep quiet—speak only when you have to.
As for the rest, I invoke Apollo
to cast his eyes down here and be my guide
when the time comes to fight it out with swords.

[Orestes, Pylades, and Electra leave together]

CHORUS

Earth brings forth many horrors—
terrors and agonies—the sea's arms
hold monsters, savage beasts.
Between the earth and heaven
hang fiery lights, suspended high.   [590]
Winged birds and beasts
that walk along the ground
can also speak of storms,
the whirlwind's power.

ἀλλ' ὑπέρτολμον ἀν-
δρὸς φρόνημα τίς λέγοι   595
καὶ γυναικῶν φρεσὶν τλαμόνων [καὶ]
παντόλμους ἔρωτας
ἄταισι συννόμους βροτῶν;
ξυζύγους δ' ὁμαυλίας
θηλυκρατὴς ἀπέρω-
τος ἔρως παρανικᾷ   600
κνωδάλων τε καὶ βροτῶν.

ἴστω δ', ὅστις οὐχ ὑπόπτερος
φροντίσιν, δαεὶς
τὰν ἁ παιδολυ-
μὰς τάλαινα Θεστιὰς μήσατο   605
πυρδαῆτιν πρόνοιαν,
καταίθουσα παιδὸς δαφοινὸν
δαλὸν ἥλικ', ἐπεὶ μολὼν
ματρόθεν κελάδησε,
ξύμμετρόν τε διαὶ βίου   610
μοιρόκραντον ἐς ἆμαρ.

ἄλλαν δεῖ τιν' ἐν λόγοις στυγεῖν
φοινίαν κόραν,
ἅτ' ἐχθρῶν ὑπαὶ   615
φῶτ' ἀπώλεσεν φίλον Κρητικοῖς
χρυσοκμήτοισιν ὅρμοις
πιθήσασα δώροισι Μίνῳ,
Νῖσον ἀθανάτας τριχὸς
νοσφίσασ' ἀπροβούλως   620
πνέονθ' ἁ κυνόφρων ὕπνῳ.
κιγχάνει δέ μιν Ἑρμῆς.

ἐπεὶ δ' ἐπεμνασάμαν ἀμειλίχων
πόνων, ὁ καιρὸς δὲ δυσφιλὲς γαμή-
λευμ' ἀπεύχετον δόμοις   625
γυναικοβούλους τε μήτιδας φρενῶν

But who of us can speak
about the arrogance of men
or women's reckless passion
beyond all self-control,
so they become conspirators
in all our lethal woes?
Passionate desire wins out—
it gains a fatal victory
in every woman.
It ends all married love   [600]
in men and beasts.

A man with any sense
should recognize these things,
once he recalls Althaea,
ruthless child of Thestius,
who planned her own son's ruin.
She burned the fatal torch,
knowing that Meleager's life,
from the time he first appeared
howling from his mother's womb,
depended on that wood.
And so it was—he stayed alive   [610]
until her fire doomed him.[8]

Another story of a hateful girl
tells of that murderous Scylla,
who killed her father,
brought to it by his enemies.
Tempted by a gift from Minos,
a golden necklace made in Crete,
she plucked out her father's hair,
the one which made Nisus immortal.
As he lay peacefully asleep,   [620]
then died, murdered by that bitch,
and Hermes led him off.[9]

As I recall these stories
of savagery without remorse,
it's time to speak of marriages
in which there was no love,
which laid a curse upon the house,
schemes devised by woman's cunning

ἐπ' ἀνδρὶ τευχεσφόρῳ,

ἐπ' ἀνδρὶ δᾴοις ἐπεικότως σέβαι.

τίω δ' ἀθέρμαντον ἑστίαν δόμων

γυναικείαν ⟨τ'⟩ ἄτολμον αἰχμάν.   630

κακῶν δὲ πρεσβεύεται τὸ Λήμνιον

λόγῳ· γοᾶται δὲ δὴ πάθος κατά-

πτυστον· ἤκασεν δέ τις

τὸ δεινὸν αὖ Λημνίοισι πήμασιν.

θεοστυγήτῳ δ' ἄχει   635

βροτῶν ἀτιμωθὲν οἴχεται γένος.

σέβει γὰρ οὔτις τὸ δυσφιλὲς θεοῖς.

τί τῶνδ' οὐκ ἐνδίκως ἀγείρω;

τὸ δ' ἄγχι πλευμόνων ξίφος

διανταίαν ὀξυπευκὲς οὐτᾷ   640

διαὶ Δίκας. τὸ μὴ θέμις γὰρ οὖν

λὰξ πέδοι πατούμενον, τὸ πᾶν Διὸς

σέβας παρεκβάντος οὐ θεμιστῶς.   645

Δίκας δ' ἐρείδεται πυθμήν·

προχαλκεύει δ' Αἶσα φασγανουργός·

τέκνον δ' ἐπεισφέρει δόμοισιν

αἱμάτων παλαιτέρων τίνειν μύσος   650

χρόνῳ κλυτὰ βυσσόφρων Ἐρινύς.

against her warrior lord, a man
his enemies have cause to honour.
I value hearth and home
where passions do not rule,
where women's spirits
rein in their waywardness.   [630]

Of all such tales of crime, the worst
concerns the isle of Lemnos,
where all the women killed their men.
At that story people moan—
they weep for that abomination.
When some new troubles come
men measure them by Lemnos.
Horror at that deed brought on
the hatred of the gods, and thus,
cast out by humankind and in disgrace,
that women's race dies out.[10]
No man can hold in reverence
what gods abhor. So of these tales
which one can I not justly cite?

Justice wields her sword.
She thrusts it home—
hungry and sharp,   [640]
it slices deep,
right by the lungs—
and so the lawlessness
of those who flout what's right,
who violate the majesty of Zeus,
lies trampled underfoot.

The anvil of Justice now holds firm.
Fate hammers out her sword—
she forges it in time.
At last the brooding Fury comes,
famous spirit of revenge—
leading a child inside the house,
to cleanse the stain of blood,   [650]
the family curse from long ago.

[Enter Orestes and Pylades, with a couple of attendants. They move up to the front doors of the royal palace. Orestes knocks loudly on the door]

ΌΡΕΣΤΗΣ

παῖ παῖ, θύρας ἄκουσον ἑρκείας κτύπον.
τίς ἔνδον, ὦ παῖ, παῖ, μάλ' αὖθις, ἐν δόμοις;
τρίτον τόδ' ἐκπέραμα δωμάτων καλῶ,   655
εἴπερ φιλόξεν' ἐστὶν Αἰγίσθου διαί.

ΟΙΚΕΤΗΣ

εἶεν, ἀκούω· ποδαπὸς ὁ ξένος; πόθεν;

ΌΡΕΣΤΗΣ

ἄγγελλε τοῖσι κυρίοισι δωμάτων,
πρὸς οὕσπερ ἥκω καὶ φέρω καινοὺς λόγους.
τάχυνε δ', ὡς καὶ νυκτὸς ἅρμ' ἐπείγεται   660
σκοτεινόν, ὥρα δ' ἐμπόρους καθιέναι
ἄγκυραν ἐν δόμοισι πανδόκοις ξένων.
ἐξελθέτω τις δωμάτων τελεσφόρος
γυνὴ τόπαρχος, ἄνδρα δ' εὐπρεπέστερον·
αἰδὼς γὰρ ἐν λεχθεῖσιν οὐκ ἐπαργέμους   665
λόγους τίθησιν· εἶπε θαρσήσας ἀνὴρ
πρὸς ἄνδρα κἀσήμηνεν ἐμφανὲς τέκμαρ.

ΚΛΥΤΑΙΜΝΗΣΤΡΑ

ξένοι, λέγοιτ' ἂν εἴ τι δεῖ· πάρεστι γὰρ
ὁποῖά περ δόμοισι τοῖσδ' ἐπεικότα,
καὶ θερμὰ λουτρὰ καὶ πόνων θελκτηρία   670
στρωμνή, δικαίων τ' ὀμμάτων παρουσία.
εἰ δ' ἄλλο πρᾶξαι δεῖ τι βουλιώτερον,
ἀνδρῶν τόδ' ἐστὶν ἔργον, οἷς κοινώσομεν

ΌΡΕΣΤΗΣ

ξένος μέν εἰμι Δαυλιεὺς ἐκ Φωκέων·
στείχοντα δ' αὐτόφορτον οἰκείᾳ σαγῇ   675
εἰς Ἄργος, ὥσπερ δεῦρ' ἀπεζύγην πόδα,
ἀγνὼς πρὸς ἀγνῶτ' εἶπε συμβαλὼν ἀνήρ,
ἐξιστορήσας καὶ σαφηνίσας ὁδόν,
Στροφίος ὁ Φωκεύς· πεύθομαι γὰρ ἐν λόγῳ
'ἐπείπερ ἄλλως, ὦ ξέν', εἰς Ἄργος κίεις,   680

54

ORESTES

    Hey, in there! You hear this knocking on the door?
    I'll try again. Anyone in there?
    All right, a third attempt. I'm knocking here—
    are you coming out? Anyone in there?
    Hello! Does Aegisthus welcome strangers?

SERVANT *[from within]*

    All right. All right. I hear you. Stranger,
    what country are you from? Who are you?

ORESTES

    Announce me to the masters of the house.
    I've come to bring them news. And hurry!   [660]
    Night's black chariot is speeding overhead.
    It's time for people on the road to rest—
    drop anchor where all strangers feel at home.
    Tell someone to come out who's in control—
    the mistress would be fine, the master
    even better. We could speak our minds.
    After all, politeness can obscure the sense.
    When we talk man to man, we get the point—
    we say just what we mean without reserve.

[Clytaemnestra and Electra enter through the palace doors]

CLYTAEMNESTRA

    Stranger, welcome. Just ask for what you need.
    Inside we have all luxuries of home—
    warm baths and beds to charm away your pains.   [670]
    We live under the eyes of Justice here.
    But if your business is more serious,
    men's work, then we'll send for Aegisthus.

ORESTES

    I'm a stranger—a Daulian from Phocis—
    coming to Argos on private business,
    carrying this pack. I need to pause and rest.
    On my way here I ran into a man—
    we'd never met before. He told me
    where he was going and asked my route.
    As we talked, I learned his name—Strophius.
    He came from Phocis, too. And he said this,
    "Well, friend, since you're heading off to Argos,   [680]

Aeschylus

πρὸς τοὺς τεκόντας πανδίκως μεμνημένος
τεθνεῶτ' Ὀρέστην εἰπέ, μηδαμῶς λάθῃ.
εἴτ' οὖν κομίζειν δόξα νικήσει φίλων,
εἴτ' οὖν μέτοικον, εἰς τὸ πᾶν ἀεὶ ξένον,
θάπτειν, ἐφετμὰς τάσδε πόρθμευσον πάλιν.   685
νῦν γὰρ λέβητος χαλκέου πλευρώματα
σποδὸν κέκευθεν ἀνδρὸς εὖ κεκλαυμένου.'
τοσαῦτ' ἀκούσας εἶπον. εἰ δὲ τυγχάνω
τοῖς κυρίοισι καὶ προσήκουσιν λέγων
οὐκ οἶδα, τὸν τεκόντα δ' εἰκὸς εἰδέναι.   690

ΚΛΥΤΑΙΜΝΗΣΤΡΑ
οἲ 'γώ, κατ' ἄκρας εἶπας ὡς πορθούμεθα.
ὦ δυσπάλαιστε τῶνδε δωμάτων Ἀρά,
ὡς πόλλ' ἐπωπᾷς, κἀκποδὼν εὖ κείμενα
τόξοις πρόσωθεν εὐσκόποις χειρουμένη,
φίλων ἀποψιλοῖς με τὴν παναθλίαν.   695
καὶ νῦν Ὀρέστης—ἦν γὰρ εὐβούλως ἔχων,
ἔξω κομίζων ὀλεθρίου πηλοῦ πόδα,—
νῦν δ' ἥπερ ἐν δόμοισι βακχείας καλῆς
ἰατρὸς ἐλπὶς ἦν, προδοῦσαν ἔγγραφε.

ΟΡΕΣΤΗΣ
ἐγὼ μὲν οὖν ξένοισιν ὧδ' εὐδαίμοσιν   700
κεδνῶν ἕκατι πραγμάτων ἂν ἤθελον
γνωστὸς γενέσθαι καὶ ξενωθῆναι· τί γὰρ
ξένου ξένοισίν ἐστιν εὐμενέστερον;
πρὸς δυσσεβείας <δ'> ἦν ἐμοὶ τόδ' ἐν φρεσίν,
τοιόνδε πρᾶγμα μὴ καρανῶσαι φίλοις,   705
καταινέσαντα καὶ κατεξενωμένον.

ΚΛΥΤΑΙΜΝΗΣΤΡΑ
οὔτοι κυρήσεις μεῖον ἀξίως σέθεν,
οὐδ' ἧσσον ἂν γένοιο δώμασιν φίλος.
ἄλλος δ' ὁμοίως ἦλθεν ἂν τάδ' ἀγγελῶν.

56

here's a message for Orestes' parents,
something they've a right to know, so please
remember it: Orestes is dead. Don't forget.
Then, when you return, you can tell me
whether his family wants to bring him back
or have him buried here in Phocis,
where he's a stranger, forever outcast.
Right now his ashes sit in a bronze urn.
The man was truly mourned." That's my message.
That's what I heard. At this point I'm not sure
whether I'm telling this to anyone who cares,
but Orestes' parent ought to be informed.   [690]

CLYTAEMNESTRA
    I . . . this news . . . what you just said . . .
    it's shattering . . . that curse we can't repress.
    It haunts the house, ranges everywhere . . .
    Someone kept safe and far away from here
    the curse seeks out. Its arrow strikes and kills.
    It takes those I love, drives me to desperation.
    And now Orestes. He was well prepared.
    He kept his feet well clear of muddy ground
    where hidden danger lurks. He offered hope
    the Furies' striking revels in this house
    might find a cure. Now, from what you say,
    we've lost that hope.

ORESTES
                    As far as I'm concerned,   [700]
    with hosts as prosperous as you, I wish
    you'd seen me as the bearer of good news
    and welcomed me for that. What's kinder
    than the link between a stranger and his host?
    But to my mind, it would have been profane
    if I'd not told his loved ones, as I promised,
    as hospitality demands.

CLYTAEMNESTRA
                            Don't worry.
    You'll receive what you deserve. In this house
    you're no less welcome for your news,
    which, in any case, someone else would bring.

Aeschylus

ἀλλ' ἔσθ' ὁ καιρὸς ἡμερεύοντας ξένους   710
μακρᾶς κελεύθου τυγχάνειν τὰ πρόσφορα.
ἄγ' αὐτὸν εἰς ἀνδρῶνας εὐξένους δόμων,
ὀπισθόπους τε τούσδε καὶ ξυνέμπορον·
κἀκεῖ κυρούντων δώμασιν τὰ πρόσφορα.
αἰνῶ δὲ πράσσειν ὡς ὑπευθύνῳ τάδε.   715
ἡμεῖς δὲ ταῦτα τοῖς κρατοῦσι δωμάτων
κοινώσομέν τε κοὐ σπανίζοντες φίλων
βουλευσόμεσθα τῆσδε συμφορᾶς πέρι.

ΧΟΡΟΣ
εἶεν, φίλιαι δμωίδες οἴκων,
πότε δὴ στομάτων   720
δείξομεν ἰσχὺν ἐπ' Ὀρέστῃ;

— ὦ πότνια χθὼν καὶ πότνι' ἀκτὴ
χώματος, ἣ νῦν ἐπὶ ναυάρχῳ
σώματι κεῖσαι τῷ βασιλείῳ,
νῦν ἐπάκουσον, νῦν ἐπάρηξον·   725
νῦν γὰρ ἀκμάζει Πειθὼ δολίαν
ξυγκαταβῆναι, χθόνιον δ' Ἑρμῆν
καὶ τὸν νύχιον τοῖσδ' ἐφοδεῦσαι
ξιφοδηλήτοισιν ἀγῶσιν.
ἔοικεν ἀνὴρ ὁ ξένος τεύχειν κακόν·   730

— τροφὸν δ' Ὀρέστου τήνδ' ὁρῶ κεκλαυμένην.
ποῖ δὴ πατεῖς, Κίλισσα, δωμάτων πύλας;
λύπη δ' ἄμισθός ἐστί σοι ξυνέμπορος;

58

But now's the time when strangers on the road   [710]
get entertained once their long journey's done.

[Clytaemnestra turns to Electra, ordering her as if she were a servant]

You there—take this traveller to the rooms
we use to entertain our guests—and with him
these fellow travellers, his attendants.
Look after them the way this house requires.
Those are my orders. See you follow them.
I'm holding you responsible. Meanwhile,
I'll go find the master of the house,
tell him the news. We don't lack friends—
from them we'll seek advice about this death.

*[Electra escorts Orestes, Pylades, and their attendants into the palace.
Clytaemnestra enters the palace. The Chorus is left alone on stage]*

CHORUS LEADER
Dear fellow slaves who serve this house,
how long before our words can demonstrate
just how strongly we support Orestes?   [720]

CHORUS
O sacred Earth,
heaped-up burial mound,
lying above that noble corpse,
commander of the ships,
hear me now,
help me now.
Now's the moment
for Persuasion to come in
with her deceit,
for that stealthy god,
Hermes of the lower world,
to guide the fight,
the fatal clash of swords.

[Enter Orestes' Nurse, Cilissa, in tears]

CHORUS LEADER
It seems the stranger's mischief is at work.   [730]
Here comes Orestes' nurse. I see she's crying.
Cilissa, why are you walking by the gates,
with your unpaid companion Sorrow?

Aeschylus

ΤΡΟΦΟΣ

Αἴγισθον ἡ κρατοῦσα τοῖς ξένοις καλεῖν
ὅπως τάχιστ᾽ ἄνωγεν, ὡς σαφέστερον   735
ἀνὴρ ἀπ᾽ ἀνδρὸς τὴν νεάγγελτον φάτιν
ἐλθὼν πύθηται τήνδε, πρὸς μὲν οἰκέτας
θετοσκυθρωπῶν ἐντὸς ὀμμάτων γέλων
κεύθουσ᾽ ἐπ᾽ ἔργοις διαπεπραγμένοις καλῶς
κείνῃ, δόμοις δὲ τοῖσδε παγκάκως ἔχειν,   740
φήμης ὕφ᾽ ἧς ἤγγειλαν οἱ ξένοι τορῶς.
ἦ δὴ κλύων ἐκεῖνος εὐφρανεῖ νόον,
εὖτ᾽ ἂν πύθηται μῦθον. ὦ τάλαιν᾽ ἐγώ·
ὥς μοι τὰ μὲν παλαιὰ συγκεκραμένα
ἄλγη δύσοιστα τοῖσδ᾽ ἐν Ἀτρέως δόμοις   745
τυχόντ᾽ ἐμὴν ἤλγυνεν ἐν στέρνοις φρένα.
ἀλλ᾽ οὔτι πω τοιόνδε πῆμ᾽ ἀνεσχόμην·
τὰ μὲν γὰρ ἄλλα τλημόνως ἤντλουν κακά·
φίλον δ᾽ Ὀρέστην, τῆς ἐμῆς ψυχῆς τριβήν,
ὃν ἐξέθρεψα μητρόθεν δεδεγμένη,—   750
κἀκ᾽ νυκτιπλάγκτων ὀρθίων κελευμάτων
καὶ πολλὰ καὶ μοχθήρ᾽ ἀνωφέλητ᾽ ἐμοὶ
τλάσῃ·—τὸ μὴ φρονοῦν γὰρ ὡσπερεὶ βοτὸν
τρέφειν ἀνάγκη, πῶς γὰρ οὔ; τρόπῳ φρενός·
οὐ γάρ τι φωνεῖ παῖς ἔτ᾽ ὢν ἐν σπαργάνοις,   755
εἰ λιμός, ἢ δίψη τις, ἢ λιψουρία
ἔχει· νέα δὲ νηδὺς αὐτάρκης τέκνων.
τούτων πρόμαντις οὖσα, πολλὰ δ᾽, οἴομαι,
ψευσθεῖσα παιδὸς σπαργάνων φαιδρύντρια,
γναφεὺς τροφεύς τε ταὐτὸν εἰχέτην τέλος.   760
ἐγὼ διπλᾶς δὲ τάσδε χειρωναξίας
ἔχουσ᾽ Ὀρέστην ἐξεδεξάμην πατρί·
τεθνηκότος δὲ νῦν τάλαινα πεύθομαι.
στείχω δ᾽ ἐπ᾽ ἄνδρα τῶνδε λυμαντήριον
οἴκων, θέλων δὲ τόνδε πεύσεται λόγον.   765

ΧΟΡΟΣ

πῶς οὖν κελεύει νιν μολεῖν ἐσταλμένον;

NURSE

My mistress ordered me to fetch Aegisthus
to meet the strangers—and to hurry up—
so he can find out clearly, man to man,
the news that's just arrived. With servants
she puts on her gloomy face, but deep down
her eyes are laughing at how well all this
has ended up for her. But for this house   [740]
the stranger's news is simply a disaster.
Once Aegisthus hears, gets the full report,
he'll jump for joy. How miserable I feel!
The old troubles of the house of Atreus,
so hard to bear, how they've hurt my heart.
I get these chest pains. But a blow like this—
I've never had to bear such sorrow.
Other troubles I've endured with patience,
but dear Orestes, how it breaks my heart!
When he was born, I got him from his mother.   [750]
I nursed him. I spent all night on my feet,
answering his cries. So much tiring work—
all for nothing. A helpless child like that
one has to nurse as if he were a beast.
How'd I do that? By following his moods.
A child in swaddling clothes can't speak at all.
So if he needed something to eat or drink,
or had just wet himself, his one response
came from his instincts. So I had to use
a prophet's skill. But often I was wrong.
I had to launder linen. Yes, I was
wet nurse and washerwoman, all in one,   [760]
two special skills. I received Orestes
from his own father's hands. Now he's dead.
That's what I've been told. It makes me cry.
Well, I must go. I have to fetch Aegisthus,
the man who brought this house to ruin.
He'll be glad enough to hear my words.

CHORUS LEADER

Did she tell him how to come and what to bring?

61

Aeschylus

ΤΡΟΦΟΣ

ἦ πῶς; λέγ' αὖθις, ὡς μάθω σαφέστερον.

ΧΟΡΟΣ

εἰ ξὺν λοχίταις εἴτε καὶ μονοστιβῆ.

ΤΡΟΦΟΣ

ἄγειν κελεύει δορυφόρους ὀπάονας.

ΧΟΡΟΣ

μή νυν σὺ ταῦτ' ἄγγελλε δεσπότου στύγει·   770
ἀλλ' αὐτὸν ἐλθεῖν, ὡς ἀδειμάντως κλύῃ,
ἄνωχθ' ὅσον τάχιστα γηθούσῃ φρενί.
ἐν ἀγγέλῳ γὰρ κυπτὸς ὀρθοῦται λόγος.

ΤΡΟΦΟΣ

ἀλλ' ἦ φρονεῖς εὖ τοῖσι νῦν ἠγγελμένοις;

ΧΟΡΟΣ

ἀλλ' εἰ τροπαίαν Ζεὺς κακῶν θήσει ποτέ.   775

ΤΡΟΦΟΣ

καὶ πῶς; Ὀρέστης ἐλπὶς οἴχεται δόμων.

ΧΟΡΟΣ

οὔπω· κακός γε μάντις ἂν γνοίη τάδε.

ΤΡΟΦΟΣ

τί φής; ἔχεις τι τῶν λελεγμένων δίχα;

ΧΟΡΟΣ

ἄγγελλ' ἰοῦσα, πρᾶσσε τἀπεσταλμένα.
μέλει θεοῖσιν ὧνπερ ἂν μέλῃ πέρι.   780

ΤΡΟΦΟΣ

ἀλλ' εἶμι καὶ σοῖς ταῦτα πείσομαι λόγοις.
γένοιτο δ' ὡς ἄριστα σὺν θεῶν δόσει.

62

NURSE

How's that? Say it again. I need a clearer sense
of what you're asking.

CHORUS LEADER

Did she tell him
to come with guards or unattended?

NURSE

She said he should bring his spearmen with him.

CHORUS LEADER

Don't give that message to Aegisthus,   [770]
that hateful tyrant. Tell him to come alone,
with a joyous heart, as quickly as he can.
He won't suspect a thing. The messenger
can straighten out a crooked message.

NURSE

What? Does your heart feel good about this news?

CHORUS LEADER

Why not, if Zeus turns evil into good?

NURSE

How's that to happen? Orestes,
the house's hope, is gone.

CHORUS LEADER

Not so fast.
A prophet who claimed that would be a bad one.

NURSE

What are you saying? Do you know something
more than what I've heard?

CHORUS LEADER

Go on then.
Relay your message. Do what you've been told.
Let the gods care about what most concerns them.   [780]

NURSE

All right, I'll go and do what you suggest.
With blessings from the gods, I pray all this
will work out for the best.

[Exit Nurse, off in search of Aegisthus, who is not in the palace]

ΧΟΡΟΣ

νῦν παραιτουμένᾳ μοι, πάτερ
Ζεῦ θεῶν Ὀλυμπίων,
δὸς τύχας τυχεῖν δόμου κυρίως   785
τὰ σώφρον’ εὖ μαιομένοις ἰδεῖν.
διὰ δίκας πᾶν ἔπος
ἔλακον· ⟨ὦ⟩ Ζεῦ, σύ νιν φυλάσσοις.

ἒ ἔ, πρὸ δὲ δὴ ’χθρῶν
τὸν ἔσωθεν μελάθρων, Ζεῦ,   790
θές, ἐπεί νιν μέγαν ἄρας,
δίδυμα καὶ τριπλᾶ
παλίμποινα θέλων ἀμείψει.

ἴσθι δ’ ἀνδρὸς φίλου πῶλον εὖ-
νιν ζυγέντ’ ἐν ἅρμασιν   795
πημάτων. ⟨σὺ δ’⟩ ἐν δρόμῳ προστιθεὶς
μέτρον κτίσον σῳζόμενον ῥυθμὸν
τοῦτ’ ἰδεῖν διὰ πέδον
ἀνομένων βημάτων ὄρεγμα;

οἵ τ’ ἔσω δωμάτων   800
πλουτογαθῆ μυχὸν νομίζετε,
κλῦτε, σύμφρονες θεοί·
[ἄγετε] τῶν πάλαι πεπραγμένων
λύσασθ’ αἷμα προσφάτοις δίκαις.
γέρων φόνος μηκέτ’ ἐν δόμοις τέκοι.   805

τὸ δὲ καλῶς κτίμενον ὦ μέγα ναίων
στόμιον, εὖ δὸς ἀνιδεῖν δόμον ἀνδρός,
καί νιν ἐλευθερίας ⟨φῶς⟩
λαμπρὸν ἰδεῖν φιλίοις
ὄμμασιν ⟨ἐκ⟩ δνοφερᾶς καλύπτρας.   810

CHORUS
   Now, in answer to my prayers,
   I implore you, Zeus,
   father of Olympian gods,
   restore this house,
   give it good fortune, so those
   who rightly love due order
   may witness it right here.
   In every word we cry,
   we plead for justice.
   O Zeus, protect what's right.

   Zeus, Zeus,
   inside that palace   [790]
   place him face to face
   before his enemies.
   If you exalt him
   he'll willingly repay you,
   three or four times over.

   You know that orphan colt,
   child of a man you cherish,
   stands now in harness,
   yoked to a chariot of pain.
   Control the way he runs,
   preserve his pace,
   so he will last the course,
   and we may see him surge,
   as he races to his goal.

   You gods inside the house,   [800]
   in those inner chambers,
   where you celebrate its wealth,
   hear me, you gods
   who sympathize with us.
   Cleanse that ancient blood
   of crimes committed long ago.
   Let old murder cease to breed.

   And Apollo, you who dwell
   in that massive well-built cavern,
   grant that this man's house
   may raise its head once more,
   so with loving eyes we see
   the veil of darkness yield   [810]
   to freedom's light.

65

Aeschylus

ξυλλάβοι δ' ἐνδίκως
παῖς ὁ Μαίας, ἐπεὶ φορώτατος
πρᾶξιν οὐρίαν θέλων·
[πολλὰ δ' ἄλλα φανεῖ χρῄζων κρυπτά].   815
ἄσκοπον δ' ἔπος λέγων
νύκτα πρό τ' ὀμμάτων σκότον φέρει,
καθ' ἡμέραν δ' οὐδὲν ἐμφανέστερος.

καὶ τότ' ἤδη κλυτὸν
δωμάτων λυτήριον,   820
θῆλυν οὐριοστάταν οὐδ'
ὀξύκρεκτον γοα-
τᾶν νόμον θήσομεν· 'πλεῖ τάδ' εὖ·
ἐμὸν ἐμὸν κέρδος αὔξεται τόδ'· ἄ-   825
τα δ' ἀποστατεῖ φίλων.'

σὺ δὲ θαρσῶν, ὅταν ἥκῃ μέρος ἔργων,
ἐπαΰσας πατρὸς αὐδὰν
θροούσᾳ [πρὸς σὲ] τέκνον [πατρὸς αὐδὰν]
[καὶ] πέραιν' ἀνεπίμομφον ἄταν.   830

Περσέως τ' ἐν φρεσὶν
καρδίαν ἀνασχεθών,
τοῖς θ' ὑπὸ χθονὸς φίλοισιν,
τοῖς τ' ἄνωθεν πρόπρασ-
σε χάριν ὀργᾶς λυγρᾶς, ἔνδοθεν   835
φόνιον ἄταν τιθείς, τὸν αἴτιον δ'
ἐξαπολλύων μόρου.

ΑΙΓΙΣΘΟΣ

ἥκω μὲν οὐκ ἄκλητος, ἀλλ' ὑπάγγελος·
νέαν φάτιν δὲ πεύθομαι λέγειν τινὰς
ξένους μολόντας οὐδαμῶς ἐφίμερον,   840

66

May Hermes, Maia's son,
support him in what's right.
He sends the finest winds
to hold an enterprise on course,
when that's his will—
and when he so desires,
he will make known
much hidden from our view,
or speak in riddles in the night,
darkening men's eyes,
which see no better by the light of day.

Soon at last we'll shout in song
of the deliverance of this house—   [820]
no shrill lament of those who mourn,
but robust songs the sea wives sing
when the wind sits fair,
"Good sailing now—for me,
for me this means more riches—
no dangers for the ones I love."

But you, Orestes, do your part—
when your moment comes, be brave.
When she cries out "My son!"
cry in return "My father's son!"
Then murder her in innocence.   [830]

In your heart maintain
the heart of Perseus.[11]
Satisfy the rage
of those you love
under the earth,
and here above.
With blood murder
inside the house
eradicate the cause
of all our blood-guilt.

[Enter Aegisthus]

AEGISTHUS
    A stranger's story called me here—
    I'm told that travellers have arrived
    with startling and unwelcome news—   [840]

67

μόρον δ' Ὀρέστου. καὶ τόδ' ἀμφέρειν δόμοις
γένοιτ' ἂν ἄχθος δειματοσταγὲς φόνῳ
τῷ πρόσθεν ἑλκαίνουσι καὶ δεδηγμένοις.
πῶς ταῦτ' ἀληθῆ καὶ βλέποντα δοξάσω;
ἢ πρὸς γυναικῶν δειματούμενοι λόγοι   845
πεδάρσιοι θρῴσκουσι, θνῄσκοντες μάτην;
τί τῶνδ' ἂν εἴποις ὥστε δηλῶσαι φρενί;

ΧΟΡΟΣ
ἠκούσαμεν μέν, πυνθάνου δὲ τῶν ξένων
ἔσω παρελθών. οὐδὲν ἀγγέλων σθένος
ὡς αὐτὸν αὐτῶν ἄνδρα πεύθεσθαι πάρα.   850

ΑΙΓΙΣΘΟΣ
ἰδεῖν ἐλέγξαι τ' αὖ θέλω τὸν ἄγγελον,
εἴτ' αὐτὸς ἦν θνῄσκοντος ἐγγύθεν παρών,
εἴτ' ἐξ ἀμαυρᾶς κληδόνος λέγει μαθών.
οὔτοι φρέν' ἂν κλέψειεν ὠμματωμένην.

ΧΟΡΟΣ
Ζεῦ Ζεῦ, τί λέγω, πόθεν ἄρξωμαι   855
τάδ' ἐπευχομένη κἀπιθεάζους',
ὑπὸ δ' εὐνοίας
    πῶς ἴσον εἰποῦσ' ἀνύσωμαι;
νῦν γὰρ μέλλουσι μιανθεῖσαι
πειραὶ κοπάνων ἀνδροδαΐκτων   860
ἢ πάνυ θήσειν Ἀγαμεμνονίων
    οἴκων ὄλεθρον διὰ παντός,
ἢ πῦρ καὶ φῶς ἐπ' ἐλευθερίᾳ
δαίων ἀρχάς τε πολισσονόμους
    πατέρων <θ'> ἕξει μέγαν ὄλβον.   865
τοιάνδε πάλην μόνος ὢν ἔφεδρος
δισσοῖς μέλλει θεῖος Ὀρέστης
    ἅψειν. εἴη δ' ἐπὶ νίκῃ.

68

Orestes is dead—yet one more burden
laid upon this house, a terrifying load,
while it still bears raw festering wounds
from earlier murder. But is what they saw
the living truth? That's what I must confirm.
Or is it some fearful women's gossip,
which blazes up, then dies away to nothing?
Can you clear my mind? What do you know?

CHORUS LEADER

Well, we heard the news. But go inside.
You can learn it from the guests themselves.
The power in a messenger's report
is not like hearing what he has to say
when you confront him face to face.   [850]

AEGISTHUS

I want to see this messenger and check
if he was present at Orestes' death,
or if he's just repeating what he heard
from some vague rumours. I'll see through him.
These keen eyes of mine won't be deceived.

[Exit Aegisthus into the palace]

CHORUS

Zeus, O Zeus,
what do I say? How do I start
appealing to the gods in prayer?
How from a loyal heart
can I find what to say,
matching words with deeds?
Now blood-stained blades
are slicing men to death   [860]
and totally destroy forever
Agamemnon's house, or else
with freedom's blazing light
Orestes wins the throne,
and all his father's riches.
The ambush now is set—
noble Orestes by himself
must face two enemies.
Let him emerge the victor!

69

ΑΙΓΙΣΘΟΣ

ἒ ἔ, ὀτοτοτοῖ.

ΧΟΡΟΣ

ἔα ἔα μάλα·   870

πῶς ἔχει; πῶς κέκρανται δόμοις;

ἀποσταθῶμεν πράγματος τελουμένου,

ὅπως δοκῶμεν τῶνδ᾽ ἀναίτιαι κακῶν

εἶναι· μάχης γὰρ δὴ κεκύρωται τέλος.

ΟΙΚΕΤΗΣ

οἴμοι, πανοίμοι δεσπότου πεπληγμένου·   875

οἴμοι μάλ᾽ αὖθις ἐν τρίτοις προσφθέγμασιν.

Αἴγισθος οὐκέτ᾽ ἔστιν. ἀλλ᾽ ἀνοίξατε

ὅπως τάχιστα, καὶ γυναικείους πύλας

μοχλοῖς χαλᾶτε· καὶ μάλ᾽ ἡβῶντος δὲ δεῖ,

οὐχ ὡς δ᾽ ἀρῆξαι διαπεπραγμένῳ· τί γάρ;   880

ἰοὺ ἰού.

κωφοῖς αὐτῶ καὶ καθεύδουσιν μάτην

ἄκραντα βάζω; ποῖ Κλυταιμήστρα; τί δρᾷ;

ἔοικε νῦν αὐτῆς ἐπὶ ξυροῦ πέλας

αὐχὴν πεσεῖσθαι πρὸς δίκην πεπληγμένος.

ΚΛΥΤΑΙΜΝΗΣΤΡΑ

τί δ᾽ ἐστὶ χρῆμα; τίνα βοὴν ἵστης δόμοις;   885

Libation Bearers

[Aegisthus screams in pain from inside the palace]

CHORUS MEMBERS *[speaking separately]*
    Listen!   [870]
                What was that?
                         What's going on,
    in there, inside the palace?

[Some members of the chorus start to move towards the palace doors]

CHORUS LEADER
    Stay back. Until this work is finished,
    we won't get involved in all the bloodshed.
    That way no one can blame us.

[A servant emerges through the palace doors]

                              It's over.
    Whatever the result, the fighting's over.

SERVANT
    Oh, it's horrible—my master's killed!
    He's dead. Alas. I'll cry it out again,
    a third time, Aegisthus is no more!

[The servant moves to a side door and tries desperately to pull it open]

    Come on! Come on! Open this door! Hurry!
    Unbolt the women's doors! A strong right arm
    is all it takes! Not to help Aegisthus—
    he's already dead. No point in trying.   [880]
    Come on! Am I shouting to the deaf,
    or are you all asleep?

[The servant gives up pounding on the side door]

                      A waste of time.
    Where's Clytaemnestra gone? What's she doing?
    Her own neck's resting on the razor's edge—
    this justice could strike her down as well.

[Enter Clytaemnestra through the main palace doors]

CLYTAEMNESTRA
    What's happening? Why are you shouting
    all around the house?

71

Aeschylus

ΟΙΚΕΤΗΣ

τὸν ζῶντα καίνειν τοὺς τεθνηκότας λέγω.

ΚΛΥΤΑΙΜΝΗΣΤΡΑ

οἲ 'γώ. ξυνῆκα τοὔπος ἐξ αἰνιγμάτων.
δόλοις ὀλούμεθ', ὥσπερ οὖν ἐκτείναμεν.
δοίη τις ἀνδροκμῆτα πέλεκυν ὡς τάχος·
εἰδῶμεν εἰ νικῶμεν, ἢ νικώμεθα·   890
ἐνταῦθα γὰρ δὴ τοῦδ' ἀφικόμην κακοῦ.

ΟΡΕΣΤΗΣ

σὲ καὶ ματεύω· τῷδε δ' ἀρκούντως ἔχει.

ΚΛΥΤΑΙΜΝΗΣΤΡΑ

οἲ 'γώ. τέθνηκας, φίλτατ' Αἰγίσθου βία.

ΟΡΕΣΤΗΣ

φιλεῖς τὸν ἄνδρα; τοιγὰρ ἐν ταὐτῷ τάφῳ
κείσῃ· θανόντα δ' οὔτι μὴ προδῷς ποτε.   895

ΚΛΥΤΑΙΜΝΗΣΤΡΑ

ἐπίσχες, ὦ παῖ, τόνδε δ' αἴδεσαι, τέκνον,
μαστόν, πρὸς ᾧ σὺ πολλὰ δὴ βρίζων ἅμα
οὔλοισιν ἐξήμελξας εὐτραφὲς γάλα.

ΟΡΕΣΤΗΣ

Πυλάδη τί δράσω; μητέρ' αἰδεσθῶ κτανεῖν;

ΠΥΛΑΔΗΣ

ποῦ δὴ τὰ λοιπὰ Λοξίου μαντεύματα   900
τὰ πυθόχρηστα, πιστὰ δ' εὐορκώματα;
ἅπαντας ἐχθροὺς τῶν θεῶν ἡγοῦ πλέον.

72

SERVANT

>   I'm telling you
> the dead are murdering the living!

CLYTAEMNESTRA

> I see. I understand your paradox.
> We're being destroyed by someone's trickery,
> just as we destroyed. All right, then,
> get me a man-killing axe—and quickly!

[Exit servant into the palace]

> Let's see now if we win through or lose.   [890]
> The wretched business brings me down to this.

[The palace doors open to reveal the dead body of Aegisthus with Orestes standing over it. Pylades is beside Orestes]

ORESTES

> The very one I seek. This fellow here
> has had enough.

CLYTAEMNESTRA

>   No, not Aegisthus,
> not my love, my power . . . dead.

ORESTES

> You loved this man? Then you'll find your rest
> in a common grave with him—he's one man
> you won't abandon when he dies.

CLYTAEMNESTRA

> Hold off, my son, my child. Take pity
> on these breasts. Here you often lay asleep.
> Your toothless gums sucked out the milk
> that made you strong.

ORESTES

>   Pylades, what do I do?
> It's a dreadful act to kill my mother.

PYLADES

> What then becomes of what Apollo said,   [900]
> what he foretold at Delphi? We made an oath.
> Make all men your enemies but not the gods.

Aeschylus

ὈΡΕΣΤΗΣ

κρίνω σὲ νικᾶν, καὶ παραινεῖς μοι καλῶς.
ἕπου, πρὸς αὐτὸν τόνδε σὲ σφάξαι θέλω.
καὶ ζῶντα γάρ νιν κρείσσον᾿ ἡγήσω πατρός·   905
τούτῳ θανοῦσα ξυγκάθευδ᾿, ἐπεὶ φιλεῖς
τὸν ἄνδρα τοῦτον, ὃν δ᾿ ἐχρῆν φιλεῖν στυγεῖς.

ΚΛΥΤΑΙΜΝΗΣΤΡΑ

ἐγώ σ᾿ ἔθρεψα, σὺν δὲ γηράναι θέλω.

ὈΡΕΣΤΗΣ

πατροκτονοῦσα γὰρ ξυνοικήσεις ἐμοί;

ΚΛΥΤΑΙΜΝΗΣΤΡΑ

ἡ Μοῖρα τούτων, ὦ τέκνον, παραιτία.   910

ὈΡΕΣΤΗΣ

καὶ τόνδε τοίνυν Μοῖρ᾿ ἐπόρσυνεν μόρον.

ΚΛΥΤΑΙΜΝΗΣΤΡΑ

οὐδὲν σεβίζῃ γενεθλίους ἀράς, τέκνον;

ὈΡΕΣΤΗΣ

τεκοῦσα γάρ μ᾿ ἔρριψας ἐς τὸ δυστυχές.

ΚΛΥΤΑΙΜΝΗΣΤΡΑ

οὔτοι σ᾿ ἀπέρριψ᾿ εἰς δόμους δορυξένους.

ὈΡΕΣΤΗΣ

αἰκῶς ἐπράθην ὢν ἐλευθέρου πατρός.   915

ΚΛΥΤΑΙΜΝΗΣΤΡΑ

ποῦ δῆθ᾿ ὁ τῖμος, ὅντιν᾿ ἀντεδεξάμην;

ὈΡΕΣΤΗΣ

αἰσχύνομαί σοι τοῦτ᾿ ὀνειδίσαι σαφῶς.

ΚΛΥΤΑΙΜΝΗΣΤΡΑ

μὴ ἀλλ᾿ εἴφ᾿ ὁμοίως καὶ πατρὸς τοῦ σοῦ μάτας.

ὈΡΕΣΤΗΣ

μὴ ᾿λεγχε τὸν πονοῦντ᾿ ἔσω καθημένη.

74

ORESTES

> That's good advice. As judge in this debate
> I say you prevail.

[Orestes turns on Clytaemnestra, pulls her towards the body of Aegisthus]

>   Over here.
> I want to kill you right beside this man.
> When he was alive, you considered him
> better than my father, so once you're dead
> you can sleep on by his side. You loved him.
> The man you should have loved you hated.

CLYTAEMNESTRA

> I brought you up. Let me grow old with you.

ORESTES

> What? Kill my father and then live with me?

CLYTAEMNESTRA

> My child, in this our fate's to blame.   [910]

ORESTES

> Then, in the same way, Fate brings on your death.

CLYTAEMNESTRA

> My son, do you not fear your mother's curse?

ORESTES

> You bore me, then threw me out to misery.

CLYTAEMNESTRA

> No, no—I sent you to live with a friend.

ORESTES

> You sold me in disgrace—a free man's son.

CLYTAEMNESTRA

> What's the price I charged for you?

ORESTES

> That's too shameful to declare in public.

CLYTAEMNESTRA

> Don't forget to name your father's failings, too.

ORESTES

> Don't charge him with anything—he worked hard
> while you sat here at home.

Aeschylus

ΚΛΥΤΑΙΜΝΗΣΤΡΑ

ἄλγος γυναιξὶν ἀνδρὸς εἴργεσθαι, τέκνον.   920

ὈΡΕΣΤΗΣ

τρέφει δέ γ᾽ ἀνδρὸς μόχθος ἡμένας ἔσω.

ΚΛΥΤΑΙΜΝΗΣΤΡΑ

κτενεῖν ἔοικας, ὦ τέκνον, τὴν μητέρα.

ὈΡΕΣΤΗΣ

σύ τοι σεαυτήν, οὐκ ἐγώ, κατακτενεῖς.

ΚΛΥΤΑΙΜΝΗΣΤΡΑ

ὅρα, φύλαξαι μητρὸς ἐγκότους κύνας.

ὈΡΕΣΤΗΣ

τὰς τοῦ πατρὸς δὲ πῶς φύγω, παρεὶς τάδε;   925

ΚΛΥΤΑΙΜΝΗΣΤΡΑ

ἔοικα θρηνεῖν ζῶσα πρὸς τύμβον μάτην.

ὈΡΕΣΤΗΣ

πατρὸς γὰρ αἶσα τόνδε σουρίζει μόρον.

ΚΛΥΤΑΙΜΝΗΣΤΡΑ

οἲ ᾽γὼ τεκοῦσα τόνδ᾽ ὄφιν ἐθρεψάμην.

ὈΡΕΣΤΗΣ

ἦ κάρτα μάντις οὑξ ὀνειράτων φόβος.
ἔκανες ὃν οὐ χρῆν, καὶ τὸ μὴ χρεὼν πάθε.   930

ΧΟΡΟΣ

στένω μὲν οὖν καὶ τῶνδε συμφορὰν διπλῆν.
ἐπεὶ δὲ πολλῶν αἱμάτων ἐπήκρισε

76

CLYTAEMNESTRA

                   My son, it's painful   [920]
for women to go on without their men.

ORESTES

Maybe, but while they stay safely in the home
their men look after them.

CLYTAEMNESTRA

My son, you really mean to do this—
to slaughter your own mother?

ORESTES

               You kill yourself.
I'll not be the murderer. You will.

CLYTAEMNESTRA

                  Take care.
The vicious hounds which avenge all mothers
will hunt you down.

ORESTES

            What about my father's?
If I don't kill you, there's no escaping them.

CLYTAEMNESTRA

It seems as if, while still alive, I waste
my useless tears at my own tomb.

ORESTES

My father's destiny has marked you out.
It states that you must die.

CLYTAEMNESTRA

               Alas for me!
You are the snake I bore and nourished.

ORESTES

Yes. That terror in your dream foretold the truth.
You killed the man you should not kill, and now   [930]
you'll suffer what no one should ever see.

[Orestes pushes Clytaemnestra inside the palace doors. Pylades goes with them. The doors close behind them]

CHORUS LEADER

The fate of these two victims makes me grieve.
But long-suffering Orestes rides the crest

77

τλήμων Ὀρέστης, τοῦθ᾽ ὅμως αἱρούμεθα,
ὀφθαλμὸν οἴκων μὴ πανώλεθρον πεσεῖν.

— ἔμολε μὲν δίκα Πριαμίδαις χρόνῳ,   935
βαρύδικος ποινά·
ἔμολε δ᾽ ἐς δόμον τὸν Ἀγαμέμνονος
διπλοῦς λέων, διπλοῦς Ἄρης.
ἔλασε δ᾽ ἐς τὸ πᾶν
ὁ πυθόχρηστος φυγὰς   940
θεόθεν εὖ φραδαῖσιν ὡρμημένος.

ἐπολολύξατ᾽ ὦ δεσποσύνων δόμων
ἀναφυγᾶς κακῶν καὶ κτεάνων τριβᾶς
ὑπαὶ δυοῖν μιαστόροιν,
δυσοίμου τύχας.

ἔμολε δ᾽ ᾧ μέλει κρυπταδίου μάχας
δολιόφρων ποινά·
ἔθιγε δ᾽ ἐν μάχᾳ χερὸς ἐτήτυμος
Διὸς κόρα—Δίκαν δέ νιν
προσαγορεύομεν βροτοὶ τυχόντες καλῶς—
ὀλέθριον πνέουσ᾽ ἐν ἐχθροῖς κότον.
<ἐπολολύξατ᾽ ὦ δεσποσύνων δόμων
ἀναφυγᾶς κακῶν καὶ κτεάνων τριβᾶς
ὑπαὶ δυοῖν μιαστόροιν,
δυσοίμου τύχας.>

τά περ ὁ Λοξίας ὁ Παρνασσίας
μέγαν ἔχων μυχὸν χθονὸς ἐπωρθία-
ξεν ἀδόλως δόλοις
βλάβαν ἐγχρονισθεῖσαν ἐποίχεται.
‘κρατεῖταί πως τὸ θεῖον παρὰ τὸ μὴ
ὑπουργεῖν κακοῖς.’
ἄξια δ᾽ οὐρανοῦχον ἀρχὰν σέβειν.   960

of so much bloodshed, we'd prefer he triumph—
the bright eyes of this house must never fade.

CHORUS
Just as justice came at last
to Priam and his sons,
a crushing retribution,
so a double lion comes
to Agamemnon's house,
a two-fold slaughter.¹²
Apollo's suppliant, the exile,   [940]
sees his action through,
driven on by justice
sent from gods above.

Raise now a shout of triumph
above our master's house,
free of misery at last,
free of that tainted couple
squandering its wealth,
and free of its unhappy fate.

He came back with a secret plan,
fighting to win crafty vengeance.
The goddess took him by the hand,
true daughter of great Zeus,
his guide throughout the fight.   [950]
Men call her rightful Justice—
who destroys her enemies
once she breathes in anger.

Raise a shout of triumph now
above our master's house,
free of misery at last,
free of that tainted couple
squandering its wealth,
free of its unhappy destiny.

From his shrine deep within the earth,
Parnassian Apollo spoke in prophecy—
"Well intentioned stealthy trickery
will conquer long-entrenched deceit."
I pray his words somehow prevail,
so I never am a slave to wickedness.
True reverence should worship heaven's rule.   [960]

πάρα τε φῶς ἰδεῖν
μέγα τ᾽ ἀφῃρέθην ψάλιον οἰκέων.
ἄναγε μὰν δόμοι· πολὺν ἄγαν χρόνον
χαμαιπετεῖς ἔκεισθ᾽ ἀεί.

τάχα δὲ παντελὴς χρόνος ἀμείψεται   965
πρόθυρα δωμάτων, ὅταν ἀφ᾽ ἑστίας
πᾶν ἐλαθῇ μύσος
καθαρμοῖσιν ἀτᾶν ἐλατηρίοις.
τύχαι δ᾽ εὐπροσωποκοῖται τὸ πᾶν
ἰδεῖν [ἀκοῦσαι] πρευμενεῖς   970
μετοίκοις δόμων πεσοῦνται πάλιν.
πάρα τε φῶς ἰδεῖν
⟨μέγα τ᾽ ἀφῃρέθην ψάλιον οἰκέων.
ἄναγε μὰν δόμοι· πολὺν ἄγαν χρόνον
χαμαιπετεῖς ἔκεισθ᾽ ἀεί.⟩

ὈΡΕΣΤΗΣ
ἴδεσθε χώρας τὴν διπλῆν τυραννίδα
πατροκτόνους τε δωμάτων πορθήτορας.
σεμνοὶ μὲν ἦσαν ἐν θρόνοις τόθ᾽ ἥμενοι,
φίλοι δὲ καὶ νῦν, ὡς ἐπεικάσαι πάθη
πάρεστιν, ὅρκος τ᾽ ἐμμένει πιστώμασι.
ξυνώμοσαν μὲν θάνατον ἀθλίῳ πατρὶ
καὶ ξυνθανεῖσθαι· καὶ τάδ᾽ εὐόρκως ἔχει.

ἴδεσθε δ᾽ αὖτε, τῶνδ᾽ ἐπήκοοι κακῶν,   980
τὸ μηχάνημα, δεσμὸν ἀθλίῳ πατρί,
πέδας τε χειροῖν καὶ ποδοῖν ξυνωρίδα.
ἐκτείνατ᾽ αὐτὸ καὶ κύκλῳ παρασταδὸν
στέγαστρον ἀνδρὸς δείξαθ᾽, ὡς ἴδῃ πατήρ,
οὐχ οὑμός, ἀλλ᾽ ὁ πάντ᾽ ἐποπτεύων τάδε   985
Ἥλιος, ἄναγνα μητρὸς ἔργα τῆς ἐμῆς,
ὡς ἂν παρῇ μοι μάρτυς ἐν δίκῃ ποτέ,
ὡς τόνδ᾽ ἐγὼ μετῆλθον ἐνδίκως μόρον

Look now, dawn is coming!
Great chains on the home are falling off.
Let this house rise up! For far too long
it's lain in pieces on the ground.

Time, which brings all things to pass,
will soon move through these doors,
once purifying rites expel
polluting evil. That will change
the roll of fortune's dice—they'll fall
so all can see the fair result,
a happy destiny once more   [970]
for all who live within the house.

Look now, dawn is coming!
Great chains on the home are falling off.
Let this house rise up! For far too long
it's lain in pieces on the ground.

*[The palace doors are thrown open, revealing Orestes standing above the bodies
of Aegisthus and Clytaemnestra. Pylades stands beside Orestes. With them are
attendants holding the bloodstained robes of Agamemnon]*

ORESTES

Here you see them—this pair of tyrants.
They killed my father, then robbed my home.
Once they sat enthroned in regal splendour.
They're lovers still, as you can witness here
by how they died, true to the oaths they swore.
They made a pact to murder my poor father,
then die together. Well, they've kept their word.

[Orestes starts unfurling the robes in which Agamemnon was killed]

Look at this again, all those of you   [980]
who pay attention to this house's troubles.
This robe they used to trap my helpless father.
With it they tied his hands and lashed his feet.
Spread it out. Stand round here in a group—
put it on display, my father's death shroud,
so that the Father (not mine—the one
who sees everything, the Sun) can see
my mother's sacrilege. Then he will come
on the day when I am judged, to testify
that I pursued and even killed my mother

81

τὸν μητρός· Αἰγίσθου γὰρ οὐ λέγω μόρον·
ἔχει γὰρ αἰσχυντῆρος, ὡς νόμος, δίκην·   990

ἥτις δ' ἐπ' ἀνδρὶ τοῦτ' ἐμήσατο στύγος,
ἐξ οὗ τέκνων ἤνεγχ' ὑπὸ ζώνην βάρος,
φίλον τέως, νῦν δ' ἐχθρόν, ὡς φαίνει, κακόν,
τί σοι δοκεῖ; μύραινά γ' εἴτ' ἔχιδν' ἔφυ
σήπειν θιγοῦσ' ἂν ἄλλον οὐ δεδηγμένον   995
τόλμης ἕκατι κἀκδίκου φρονήματος.

τί νιν προσείπω, κἂν τύχω μάλ' εὐστομῶν;
ἄγρευμα θηρός, ἢ νεκροῦ ποδένδυτον
δροίτης κατασκήνωμα; δίκτυον μὲν οὖν,
ἄρκυν τ' ἂν εἴποις καὶ ποδιστῆρας πέπλους.   1000
τοιοῦτον ἂν κτήσαιτο φηλήτης ἀνήρ,
ξένων ἀπαιόλημα κἀργυροστερῆ
βίον νομίζων, τῷδέ τ' ἂν δολώματι
πολλοὺς ἀναιρῶν πολλὰ θερμαίνοι φρένα.
τοιάδ' ἐμοὶ ξύνοικος ἐν δόμοισι μὴ
γένοιτ'· ὀλοίμην πρόσθεν ἐκ θεῶν ἄπαις.

ΧΟΡΟΣ

αἰαῖ ⟨αἰαῖ⟩ μελέων ἔργων·
στυγερῷ θανάτῳ διεπράχθης.
ἒ ἔ,
μίμνοντι δὲ καὶ πάθος ἀνθεῖ.

ΟΡΕΣΤΗΣ

ἔδρασεν ἢ οὐκ ἔδρασε; μαρτυρεῖ δέ μοι   1010
φᾶρος τόδ', ὡς ἔβαψεν Αἰγίσθου ξίφος.
φόνου δὲ κηκὶς ξὺν χρόνῳ ξυμβάλλεται,
πολλὰς βαφὰς φθείρουσα τοῦ ποικίλματος.
νῦν αὐτὸν αἰνῶ, νῦν ἀποιμώζω παρών,
πατροκτόνον θ' ὕφασμα προσφωνῶν τόδε.   1015

in a just cause. About Aegisthus' death
there's nothing I need say. As an adulterer,   [990]
he dies—our law's just punishment.

But as for her who planned this evil act
against her husband, a man whose children
she carried in her womb—I loved her once,
but she became my bitter enemy,
as you can see. What do you make of her?
If she'd been born a viper or sea snake,
she wouldn't need to bite—her very touch
would make men rot, so evil is her heart,
so reckless.

[Orestes stoops and picks up the bloody robe]

What do I call this?
What fine words will do? A snare for some wild beast?
A corpse's shroud? The curtain from a bath
wrapped round his legs? No. It's a hunting net.
That name sounds right—robes to trap a man,   [1000]
entangling his feet, something a highway thief
might use to trick and rob a stranger.
With such a net he'd take so many lives,
his pleasure in the work would warm his heart.
May I never live with such a woman.
Before that, let the gods destroy me—
let me die without a child.

CHORUS
Alas for this horrific act,
the monstrous way she died.
But woe on the survivor, too—
his suffering begins to flower.

ORESTES
Did she commit the crime or not? Come here.   [1010]
This clothing is my witness, dyed with blood.
It's from Aegisthus' blade. These bloody stains
with time have blotted out the fine embroidery.
But I can praise my father. Now at last
I'm here to mourn him, as I hold this robe,
the net that brought about my father's death.
But I lament my act, my suffering.

83

ἀλγῶ μὲν ἔργα καὶ πάθος γένος τε πᾶν,
ἄζηλα νίκης τῆσδ' ἔχων μιάσματα.

ΧΟΡΟΣ

οὔτις μερόπων ἀσινὴς βίοτον
διὰ παντὸς ἀπήμον' ἀμείψει.
ἒ ἔ,
μόχθος δ' ὁ μὲν αὐτίχ', ὁ δ' ἥξει.   1020

ΟΡΕΣΤΗΣ

ἀλλ', ὡς ἂν εἰδῆτ', οὐ γὰρ οἶδ' ὅπη τελεῖ,
ὥσπερ ξὺν ἵπποις ἡνιοστροφῶ δρόμου
ἐξωτέρω· φέρουσι γὰρ νικώμενον
φρένες δύσαρκτοι· πρὸς δὲ καρδίᾳ φόβος
ᾄδειν ἕτοιμος ἠδ' ὑπορχεῖσθαι κότῳ.   1025
ἕως δ' ἔτ' ἔμφρων εἰμί, κηρύσσω φίλοις
κτανεῖν τέ φημι μητέρ' οὐκ ἄνευ δίκης,
πατροκτόνον μίασμα καὶ θεῶν στύγος.
καὶ φίλτρα τόλμης τῆσδε πλειστηρίζομαι
τὸν πυθόμαντιν Λοξίαν, χρήσαντ' ἐμοὶ   1030
πράξαντι μὲν ταῦτ' ἐκτὸς αἰτίας κακῆς
εἶναι, παρέντα δ'—οὐκ ἐρῶ τὴν ζημίαν·
τόξῳ γὰρ οὔτις πημάτων ἐφίξεται.

καὶ νῦν ὁρᾶτέ μ', ὡς παρεσκευασμένος
ξὺν τῷδε θαλλῷ καὶ στέφει προσίξομαι   1035
μεσόμφαλόν θ' ἵδρυμα, Λοξίου πέδον,
πυρός τε φέγγος ἄφθιτον κεκλημένον,
φεύγων τόδ' αἷμα κοινόν· οὐδ' ἐφ' ἑστίαν
ἄλλην τραπέσθαι Λοξίας ἐφίετο.
καὶ μαρτυρεῖν μὲν ὡς ἐπορσύνθη κακὰ
τάδ' ἐν χρόνῳ μοι πάντας Ἀργείους λέγω·

I mourn the entire race, for though I've won,
I can't avoid the guilt which now pollutes me.

CHORUS
No mortal goes through life unscathed,
free from pain until the end.
One trouble comes today,
yet another comes tomorrow.   [1020]

ORESTES *[starting to break down]*
But still, you need to understand . . .
I don't know how this will end . . . I feel like
some chariot racer lashing on my team,
but we're way off track . . . My mind is racing . . .
it's lost control. Something's overpowering me . . .
carrying me off . . . Deep in my heart, fear
prepares its furious song and dance.
So while I still have my wits about me,
to all my friends I publicly proclaim
I killed my mother not without just cause.
She was guilty of my father's murder,
a woman gods despised. What drove me on?
I cite as my chief cause the Delphic prophet,   [1030]
Apollo's priest, who said this to me,
"If you carry out this act, you'll go free—
no charge of evil. But if you refuse . . ."
I won't describe the punishment—
no arrow fired from a bow could reach
the top of so much pain.

[Pylades hands Orestes an olive branch, the mark of a suppliant to Apollo's oracle at Delphi]

                         Look at me now—
armed with this branch and wreath, I go
a suppliant to earth's central navel stone,
Apollo's realm, to that sacred flame
which, people say, never dies away,
an exile who murdered his own blood.
Apollo's prophet gave me his orders—
I'm to go to his shrine, no other place.
As to how I did this brutal act,
I call all men of Argos—be my witnesses   [1040]
to Menelaus when he comes back home.

ἐγὼ δ' ἀλήτης τῆσδε γῆς ἀπόξενος,
ζῶν καὶ τεθνηκὼς τάσδε κληδόνας λιπών.

ΧΟΡΟΣ

　ἀλλ' εὖ γ' ἔπραξας, μηδ' ἐπιζευχθῇς στόμα
　φήμῃ πονηρᾷ μηδ' ἐπιγλωσσῶ κακά,
　ἐλευθερώσας πᾶσαν Ἀργείων πόλιν,
　δυοῖν δρακόντοιν εὐπετῶς τεμὼν κάρα.

ΟΡΕΣΤΗΣ

　ἆ, ἆ.
　δμωαὶ γυναῖκες, αἵδε Γοργόνων δίκην
　φαιοχίτωνες καὶ πεπλεκτανημέναι
　πυκνοῖς δράκουσιν· οὐκέτ' ἂν μείναιμ' ἐγώ.　　　　1050

ΧΟΡΟΣ

　τίνες σε δόξαι, φίλτατ' ἀνθρώπων πατρί,
　στροβοῦσιν; ἴσχε, μὴ φόβου νικῶ πολύ.

ΟΡΕΣΤΗΣ

　οὐκ εἰσὶ δόξαι τῶνδε πημάτων ἐμοί·
　σαφῶς γὰρ αἵδε μητρὸς ἔγκοτοι κύνες.

ΧΟΡΟΣ

　ποταίνιον γὰρ αἷμά σοι χεροῖν ἔτι·　　　　1055
　ἐκ τῶνδέ τοι ταραγμὸς ἐς φρένας πίτνει.

ΟΡΕΣΤΗΣ

　ἄναξ Ἄπολλον, αἵδε πληθύουσι δή,
　κἀξ ὀμμάτων στάζουσιν αἷμα δυσφιλές.

ΧΟΡΟΣ

　εἷς σοι καθαρμός· Λοξίας δὲ προσθιγὼν
　ἐλεύθερόν σε τῶνδε πημάτων κτίσει.　　　　1060

86

Remember me in years to come. Now I go,
wandering in exile from my country.
Whether I live or die, I leave with you
your memory of me.

CHORUS LEADER

But you've done great things.
Why depress your spirit with such talk,
ominous predictions, evil omens?
You've freed the city, all of Argos,
hacking off the heads of those two serpents,
a healing blow.

[Orestes is suddenly overpowered with fear by a vision of his mother's Furies coming after him]

ORESTES

No . . . They're here . . .
Look, you women . . . over there . . .
like Gorgons draped in black . . . their heads
hundreds of writhing snakes . . .   [1050]
I can't stand it here . . .

CHORUS LEADER

What's wrong? What are you looking at?
Of all men you have a father's strongest love,
so stay calm. Don't give in to fear

ORESTES

It's no imagined horror, no!
It's real. Out there my mother's blood hounds wait.
They want revenge.

CHORUS LEADER

Your hands are still blood stained—
that's made your mind disordered.

ORESTES

Lord Apollo!
They come at me! Hordes of them! Their eyes
drip blood . . . it's horrible!

CHORUS LEADER

There's just one cure—
Apollo's touch will cleanse you, set you free   [1060]
of these hallucinations.

87

Aeschylus

ΟΡΕΣΤΗΣ
  ὑμεῖς μὲν οὐχ ὁρᾶτε τάσδ', ἐγὼ δ' ὁρῶ·
  ἐλαύνομαι δὲ κοὐκέτ' ἂν μείναιμ' ἐγώ.

ΧΟΡΟΣ
  ἀλλ' εὐτυχοίης, καί σ' ἐποπτεύων πρόφρων
  θεὸς φυλάσσοι καιρίοισι συμφοραῖς.

— ὅδε τοι μελάθροις τοῖς βασιλείοις   1065
  τρίτος αὖ χειμὼν
      πνεύσας γονίας ἐτελέσθη.
  παιδοβόροι μὲν πρῶτον ὑπῆρξαν
  μόχθοι τάλανές [τε Θυέστου]·
  δεύτερον ἀνδρὸς βασίλεια πάθη·   1070
  λουτροδάικτος δ' ὤλετ' Ἀχαιῶν
  πολέμαρχος ἀνήρ·
  νῦν δ' αὖ τρίτος ἦλθέ ποθεν σωτήρ,
  ἢ μόρον εἴπω;
  ποῖ δῆτα κρανεῖ, ποῖ καταλήξει   1075
      μετακοιμισθὲν μένος ἄτης;

ORESTES

You don't see them. I do.

They're coming for me. I have to leave . . .

[Orestes runs off. Pylades follows him]

CHORUS LEADER

Good fortune go with you. And may god
watch over you, protect you with his favours.

CHORUS

The third storm has broken on the palace,
then run its course across the royal clan.
First, came the torments of those children
slaughtered for Thyestes' food.[13] Next came   [1070]
the suffering of a man, our warrior lord,
Achaea's king. And now the third—
do I call him our saviour or our doom?
When will all this cease? When will murder,
its fury spent, rest at last in sleep?

NOTES

1.   Thyestes, the father of Aegisthus, was the brother of Atreus, the father of Agamemnon and Menelaus.

2.   Hermes, a divine son of Zeus, accompanied the dead down to Hades.

3.   The Furies are the goddesses of blood revenge, particularly within the family.

4.   Atreus was the father of Agamemnon and Menelaus.

5.   The Scamander was the river near Troy, the site of many battles in the Trojan War.

6.   Persephone is the queen of the underworld, wife of Hades.

7.   Pelops was the original founder of the royal family of Argos.

8.   Althaea was the mother of Meleager. When he was born, the Fates told her that Meleager would live as long as a log in the fireplace. Althaea removed the log and preserved it to keep Meleager alive. However, when Meleager, in an angry fit, killed Althaea's two brothers, she threw the log in the fire and killed her son.

9.   Nisus had a purple lock of hair on which the safety of his kingdom depended. When Minos, king of Crete, besieged their city, Scylla, daughter of the king, cut off her father's lock and presented it to Minos, who promptly abandoned her.

10. The women of Lemnos offended the goddess Aphrodite, who, in revenge gave them all a dreadful smell. When the men of Lemnos started sleeping with other women, the wives on the island killed their husbands.

11. Perseus, a son of Zeus, was a famous hero, who, among other things, killed the Gorgon Medusa, whose gaze turned people to stone.

12. Priam was king of Troy, killed when the city was ransacked at the end of the Trojan War.

13. Thyestes, father of Aegisthus, was a brother of Atreus and thus uncle of Agamemnon. Atreus had killed Thyestes' two sons and served them to him at what was supposed to be a feast of reconciliation. Aegisthus' murder of Agamemnon is his revenge for those killings.

www.ingramcontent.com/pod-product-compliance
Lightning Source LLC
Chambersburg PA
CBHW060941040426
42445CB00011B/960